Author: D. Preme Norman

Cover Design: A Pen in the Pen Publishing, LLC

Typesetting: A Pen in the Pen Publishing, LLC

Edited by: KBang

www.peninthpen.com

Twitter: @DPremeNorman

Table of Contents

DEDICATION

*This book is dedicated to the fire that purified me for 46 years! My biological father, Luther Z. Norman. I love & miss you Pop! I finally did it! Rest in Peace!

*Arkell M. Spencer II & Mildred E Spencer. I love & miss y'all so much!!! May they rest in peace in a glorious seat next to the throne of God! Thank you for overseeing me through all of my past trials and tribulations... Thank you for being Romans chapter 8 when I was Romans chapter 7. God has me now! Rest up!

*Mom & Dad: Be joyful always; pray continually; continue to give thanks in all circumstances. For it is God's will for you (us) in Christ Jesus! You guys have given me a gorgeous example of how to overcome the trials and tribulations. Y'all are great parents as well as individuals in Christ.

*Dad (Robert)...may we challenge each other to live in the Temple with Boaz & Jakin strength & establishment, as well as unlock the mysteries of greatness "together" finally. Let us abandon ourselves to the grace & will of God so that we may be enthralled with him both now and forever!

*Mom (Pat)...My Queen... Thank you for giving me a living example of the Grace & Mercy of God and the joy of the Lord (as a believer's strength) and may we challenge each other to live this life of joy and grow our hearts in faith and Thanksgiving!

FOREWORD

YOUNG BROTHERS, IT TOOK US MULTIPLE TRIPS TO HELL AND BACK, YEARS OF STRUGGLE AND ADVERSITY, AN ABUNDANCE OF FAILURES, AND LOSSES OF PRECIOUS TIME THAT WE CAN NEVER GET BACK TO COME TO THIS AWAKENING MOMENT. THE BROTHER D. PREME'S SOLE PURPOSE FOR WRITING THIS MANUSCRIPT IS TO SEE TO IT THAT HISTORY DOESN'T REPEAT ITSELF WITH YOU YOUNG BROTHERS AND SISTERS. HE IS NOT WRITING THIS FOR FINANCIAL GAIN OR SOCIAL RECOGNITION, BUT OUT OF GENUINE CONCERN FOR THOSE COMING UP AFTER US WHO ARE HEADED DOWN A PATH OF DESTRUCTION WITHOUT BEING CONSCIOUS OF WHAT ACTUALLY LIES BEFORE THEM. HE'S GOING TO GIVE YOU GUYS A DETAILED DESCRIPTION OF WHAT YOU SUBJECT YOURSELVES TO WHEN YOU CHOOSE TO LIVE LIFE THE WAY THAT WE LIVED IT AT YOUR AGE. THIS BOOK IS RAW AND UNCUT AND WILL DISPLAY ALL OF THE HARSH PENALTIES THAT COME WITH CHOOSING THE STREETS TO BE YOUR PLAYGROUND, FROM BEING FACED WITH JAIL AND DEATH ON MANY OCCASIONS, TO TONS OF MISSED OPPORTUNITIES. HE WILL ALSO SHOW YOU HOW YOU CAN DEFY THE ODDS AND BECOME MORE THAN JUST A STATISTIC. NO MATTER WHAT YOU'VE ALREADY BEEN THROUGH, THIS WILL SHOW YOU HOW TO TURN STRUGGLE, ADVERSITY, FAILURE AND LOSS INTO POSITIVE GROWTH, DEVELOPMENT, WINDOWS OF OPPORTUNITY, AND THE ULTIMATE LEVEL OF MATURATION. IF YOU KNOW DEEP DOWN INSIDE OF YOU THAT YOU ARE ON A DESTRUCTIVE PATH, THEN TURN THE PAGE AND FIND

OUT THE COST OF YOUR ACTIONS AND HOW YOU CAN DEFY THE STATISTICS AND BECOME MORE THAN JUST A NUMBER!

-K.BANG*

INTRODUCTION

During such an interesting sequence of my life in which there were an abundance of temptations, tribulations and failures that I had succumbed to, I wanted to take an authentic and nontraditional approach in writing this book. So in penning this manuscript, what strictly came to heart and mind was the life of a higher being in the soul of man!

I am convinced that the cause of many of life's failures for minorities is, some of us lack the proper gratitude necessary for our Higher Power and the humility, wisdom and unity in our lives. Without knowledge it is impossible to experience appreciation for anything we cannot embrace in high esteem; something (or someone) of which you know not. It is virtually impossible to value that which you are not aware of! For example: if you are not aware of the marvels of Black or African History, you cannot properly appreciate these disciplines. If you don't know or are perhaps not aware of your place in community and family structure, you cannot appreciate it... If you don't know or perhaps aren't aware of God's presence in your life or your worth as a King or Queen than you cannot appreciate none of the above, nor benefit from your historical value and God's greatness. You cannot properly appreciate the "Giver of life" or the "Gift of life" when lacking knowledge of either.

I wrote this book, because our future is made for us by historical texts. Since sin tries to destroy us, virtue in righteousness protects us and ensures betterment in our future! In this world, the purity of man and woman's love is so under educated that because so, they seek to do work of destruction instead of productivity.

Since the fall of Adam, man has been a caricature of himself. This calamity happens because we develop this thing called "Pride"! Sadly, we begin to exalt ourselves as masters of our own universe. Essentially, we move to certain areas of our lives trying to dethrone reality by not seeing things as we are, but as we become.

1

All too often, instead of trusting the inner-wisdom--that natural genius inside--most people follow the crowd. We do things because everybody does it.

If we pay attention to history, there are 2 things that are quite profound; the story teller and the person whom was there to listen/receive the story. We become the stories we listen to (parents, friends, books, news, social media, etc...). However, the Creator's plan is for us to become a better version of ourselves. The people we encounter, the stories we listen to, the books we read, etc.; have they impacted our lives? If so, how? That movie we watched, did it dig into the depths of our soul? That song that we listened to, did it move us to inspire in a way that is parallel with harmonious love and peace?

I wrote this book also for those who may have been stuck in an emotional whirlwind of anger, sadness, depression, fear, etc, etc... The problem is not in that whirlwind of emotions, but in not dealing with these emotions properly and allowing them to have counterproductive effects on our behaviors.

Until we are able to see who we are in every room we enter, those in the rooms control the doors in which you exit!

Who are you? At the bottom of our intellect, physical and mental prowess--beyond the lady-getter, money-getter, the gangster, the gang-banger (women as well), beyond the emotional neediness, LIES A TRUTH!

One final question: What is the difference between the life you're living and the life you want to live???

LOST SOULS (PART II)

THEY DON'T SEE THINGS AS THEY ACTUALLY ARE, ONLY AS THEY APPEAR TO BE,

BUT IF YOU SAID THIS TO ONE OF THOSE LOST SOUL, THEY WOULD STRONGLY DISAGREE...

THEIR MOUTHS ARE OPEN, BUT THEIR EARS ARE CLOSED. THEY THINK THEY KNOW IT ALL.

GROWTH AND DEVELOPMENT IS HARD FOR THEM, BECAUSE THEY CAN'T EVEN SEE THEIR FLAWS!!!

SHORT TEMPERED. HARD-HEADED, AND IN A RUSH TO PLEASE THEIR FRIENDS.

THEY FAIL TO REALIZE THAT WHAT THEY CONSIDER A FRIEND IS NOT A FRIEND...

GREED AND HATE ARE COMMON SINS, BUT FOR THEM YOU CAN TIMES IT BY TEN!

THE GIRLS THINK THEY ARE WOMEN, AND THE BOYS THINK THEY ARE MEN...

THEY MAY HAVE MONEY, THEY MAY HAVE FAME, BUT WITHOUT IT THEY HAVE NOTHING!

THEY TALK ABOUT NONSENSE, BUT BETTERMENT IS NOT SOMETHING THEY ENJOY DISCUSSING...

MENTALLY, THEY ARE FAR BEHIND, BUT LET THEM TELL IT, THEY'RE WINNING,

AND THEY'RE COMPLETELY IN DENIAL ABOUT THE DESTRUCTIVE LIFESTYLES THEY ARE LIVING...

WHEN IT COMES TIME TO REAP WHAT THEY'VE SOWN, THEY CAN'T TAKE WHAT THEY'VE GIVEN.

BUT IF THEY WEREN'T LOST, THEY WOULD HAVE PREPARED THEMSELVES IN THE VERY BEGINNING...

THEY SAY THEY LOVE THE CLOSEST PEOPLE TO THEM, BUT THEY DON'T EVEN LOVE THEMSELVES.

THAT LOVE IS THE KIND OF LOVE THAT NEVER ENDS WELL...

I'M ABLE TO DISECT THESE LOST SOULS, BECAUSE I WAS ONE MYSELF!

WHEN I FOUND OUT, I KILLED MYSELF AND GREW INTO SOMEONE ELSE...

-K-BANG*

CHAPTER I

GENESIS (WHO AM I?)

Realistically and statistically provided, with Black, Hispanics, i.e., "The Hood", everything is a numbers game! Monetary, materialistic and a need to always keep up with the Joneses are traits that majority of The Hood possess, which keeps us in The Hood and prevents us from overcoming our hardships. Due to a lack of financial education in Black Communities, we suffered greatly, and still we suffer! It has been an arduous task to reconstruct what has been inequivalently constructed so long ago. When our brothers and sisters did attempt to recondition their minds, and build a community that pooled its resources, that community was literally destroyed and no one was penalized for that destruction. This community that I speak of was in Tulsa Oklahoma and was called "Black Wall St.". The late Great Isaac Montgomery, an African American teacher of Black economics, played a pivotal role in that Reconstruction Era by enhancing the awareness of his people in an economical sense which was key to bringing forth Black Wall St. This was the first all "Black owned" community, having their own stores, banks, law enforcement, nurses, doctors, etc. It shouldn't take much wondering to see why the Blacks whom know about this historical event haven't attempted to create a Black Wall St. of their own. The entire community was literally torched, burned to the ground, and only because the occupants of Black Wall St. had become independent and no longer needed the unhelping hand of a white man.

*****

1986, I returned back home from an accumulative 4 year stint in an adolescent facility called "Summerset Hills", in quiet Warren County, North New Jersey. This period of restricted confinement was clearly the result of my violation of a congruous court-order, previously related to behaviors that were anything other than heroic.

Prior to the above, 1982, I'd spent 28 days in a facility called T.R.I.S.S (Don't bother to fix your brain to ask in curiosity what the acronym stands for, because I don't even know, nor do I care to remember). However, considering the fact of both, I learned not one thing--they were ineffective! If in fact these said institutions/programs were geared and structured for educational and therapeutic attainment, I myself along with over 2 million others would not occupy these institutional slave markets as I pen my truth through these paper lines! What I'm talking about here is this government play to further their crooked agendas and declare war on our men, women and youth!

Like Fredrick Douglas, I would have discovered why "Master" tried to keep me illiterate to these private/government invested securities. My brain was clearly not properly prepared to embrace the realistic terms these government facilities provided, the illegitimate purpose they possessed for my Black life! In all reality and in retrospect, not too much of anything that was taught through those institutions/programs and schools for any matter, meant anything to me, or were really even remembered when I was emancipated from the Security Branch. We are all Commodities (chattel) in this corporate place they call a country, the U.S.A. Security(s) is: an obligation of a person or a share participation or other interest in a person or a property or an enterprise of a person which is or is of a type of trade or financial market... Does this not sound historically familiar?!? And we wonder why people of color are identified as and represented by numbers and institutions instead of the natural Law of God and Liberty. Now, how do we continue to succumb to this political, economic, and racial scheme?!?

At the age of 14, I now had served mental, emotional and physical time in places of no purpose. Having done so, chief within me lie *ebullition*, understanding a lie of twisted pathological ideology in order to get by.

I've spent numerous of hours and years in the unwanted company of youths from many different walks of life. The cities they were from and homes they grew up in were evident in their diction. It is

6

said that we become the soul product of the exact environment in which we dwell. Therefore, this considerable amount of time trapped in this idiom heightened my need to be, fueling my pseudointellect to build this "somebody". In considering the mental capacity, my strengths or weaknesses can cause such an unparalleled sense of unwanted notoriety.

I was an entirely blessed (inamorato) creature in the System of God! Not aware of my executive position in His Branch, I ended up submitting to *malversation*. Image was just as imperative to me as hygiene was to one who had *hygeiolatry*. When I woke up in the morning, champion in me was to impress! So I draped myself in the necessities that attracted my target audience, the women and the injurious role models that I looked up to. What real dude doesn't like comments that feed and build the ego? I was my father, "Louie's", son! The love for women back then was apparent. I was all in when it came to putting on for the ladies and well put together for my age might I say. My vernacular was fair. I was about 6'2, 200 lbs., charming, quite manipulative, very convincing and confident, idyllic, humble and reserved. In the 80's (my teens), I was like Lebron James in his prime! Having a physical frame that was such, it made it that much easier to take part in my pathological express. In essence, I had the 48 Laws of Power and Art of War intelligence without even laying eyes on the books. The fact that I was living in a state of *adonization* didn't help either. Being conscious of my abilities to perform certain tasks, this, nonetheless was predicated on the scope of how the opposite viewed me and made a total assessment of what and who I am, instead of who I should really be!

Back in my youth, if your mother worked enough overtime at her first job, or if you had a father (which a vast majority of my peers didn't have) that worked enough, you were lucky to get an official bike for Christmas, and just any bike. I'm talking about the name brand bikes, like a Haro, Mongoose, or a Kaharah with the stunt pegs... If you weren't fortunate enough to have afforded one, then the next best option was to go to one of the more affluent neighborhoods and steal one. Parents were no help, mothers would see to it that kids went to school looking like a million bucks, just so she could say to whoever was paying attention, "That's my son with the $125 sneakers and $75 jeans on..." Yeah, an average mother from the hood will spend money that is supposed to be saved or spent on something more important on making sure her son doesn't make her look bad or keeping up with the joneses, and all the while she's back on her rent, her credit cards are maxed out and food is scarce. So you see, it is no wonder why we grow up not knowing the value of a dollar and keeping up with the joneses is more important than paying your bills on time, good credit and saving money.

So many of our own have been excluded from advancement and have succumbed to zero growth and economic oppression. This dire circumstance brings forth the reality of numbers not adding up in their households. Left in the most difficult state, a young gamin has to produce the financial means that cease to exist. In saying all of the above, a lot of what I saw or didn't see growing up began to mold me and shape my belief systems.

At my feet were chances to prosper in many financial ventures that I had never encountered before. Granted, my upbringing wasn't a terrible one. Ugly at times, but manageable. My mother educated herself very hard despite our lowest points in life. Hard worker, intelligent, very beautiful, 5 foot 3 with a smile that highly illuminated every space that her God-gifted presence entered. Like many Black women from stressful urban socio-economic circumstances, my mother struggled to make ends meet and had personal issues of her own that she surrendered to. However, she always persisted in her wisdom, teaching things to me and my sister, 'Nae'; anyone for that matter.

My step-father, he was different than most Black brothers I knew! I couldn't really make light of his differences though. In fact, if you want me to be honest, I hated him sometimes! This is one of the instances where my ego and pride got in the way of my growth. I never understood him, because my ego, pride and hard-headedness wouldn't allow me to. He was a disciplinarian, a man that abnegated the things of the world for the sake of his family. 6 foot 3, about

230 lbs., skin as pure as fresh black coffee, and very intelligent, rooted in the seeds of enormous wisdom. He was also tremendously handy, could fix anything around the house. I was actually under his tutelage in a general sense. He worked for Gloucester County Jail with the rank of a Sergeant, but he had the leadership skills of a General! In retrospect, he loved me unconditionally and embraced me as his son, as a man of God loves his son, which calls to mind this scripture:

Psalm (2:7-11) "I will proclaim the Lord's decree; He said   to me, you are my son; today I have become your father. Ask   me and I will make the nations your inheritance, the ends   of the earth your possession. You will break them with a   rod of iron, you will dash them to pieces like pottery.   Therefore, you King be wise; be warned, you rulers of the   earth. Serve the lord with fear and celebrate his rejoice   with trembling...."

In the sense that God is our Creator, all of us are His children, but the King had a unique relationship with God based on what God had assigned him. In biblical times the Davidic King was the Lord's servant and son. My father held high regards for me and realized and recognized the potential in me that I wasn't conscious enough to see myself. He saw the King in me as God saw, but I was so *unasinous* that I was out of view of the opportunity to fully *under grope* what lay right before me.

How was I blind to this social identity that was taking place and ethnic identity itself that was fluid and malleable? Some type of capitalism is going on!

Until the rise of Market Capitalism, wage labor, the Protestant Ethnicity, Private Property, and possessive individualism, kinship connections had operated as a major indices that gave all peoples a sense of who they were. Even in the most technologically and politically advanced societies of the ancient world such as, Rome, kinship was the important diacritic of connectedness to the social system. In all of the most patriarchal societies of the middle east,

9

Africa and the Mediterranean, the average person was identified by who his or her father was. The long list of names of who begat whom in The Old Testament of the bible (Book of Genesis) attests to importance, especially at the tribal and chiefdom levels of genealogical identity.

Another important diagnostic of identity was occupation. Whether one was a farmer, carpenter, fisherman, tanner, brass worker, herdsman, philosopher, government official, poet, healer, warrior, or even a harlot (prostitute). Yes, even a harlot was significantly salient in the eyes of the ancient world. All of these titles are what made society and gave identities. Occupants determined to some extent how people were viewed and treated as well as underscored.

The Bible says, "...Honor thy mother and thy father..." And in traditional customs, it took a village to raise a child, and that child grew up to be responsible, blessed, prestigious and ceremonial; honor was brought--wisdom and strength was built.

So why did I not honor my mother nor my father?

*****

September 1986, a small amount of my associates and peers began to indulge in the drug game, and some advanced in the game beyond anything I ever imagined. Unbeknownst to my cognizance, this was the beginning of what was later labeled "The Crack Era"! When crack/cocaine hit the streets, it was an epidemic like no other, and people around me were coming up from it. Right before my eyes, my associates were transforming overnight. One day they were eating assisted lunch meals that the school provided and wearing Payless shoes and thrift store clothes. Then, next thing you know they have 3 to $400 in their pockets, Ellessee's, Lee suites, leather fronts and they were buying lunch for everybody with those extra pies, cakes and donuts no one could afford.

I was extremely athletic in sports. So I excelled in basketball and football. At the time, I was highly publicized. My versatility stood the test in sports. Coaches witnessed my potential on the field. I took part in the pop warner football as a youth. My physical structure demanded attention! So I was extensively aggressive in competing. Anyway, I was into football heavy! On defense, I hit like a bull, and on offense, I'd try to run you over like a train. Eric Dickerson, who played for the LA Rams, a 6 foot 3 running back, was one of my favorite players. I wanted to be just like him. Ronni Lott, who played for the San Francisco 49ers, was a 6 foot 3 safety, and he was the meanest brother that ever played the position. He was known for his damaging hits. Well, my Pops posted me to be better than him. He coached me through a lot of practices, or at least he tried to, but the images of my associates now acquiring the wealth that the drug trade provided continued to torment my psyche, igniting a desire to want what they had.

At this point, my BMX competing days were about to slowly fade out, which I regretted due to my expertise in it. 1984 I began a quest in the sport of BMXing. My mother thought that it may be just a phase that I was experiencing since I was into all of the other things kids are into that parents think to be weird. You want to know the funny thing about all of this? As I showed up every week to race against the masses of white privileged adolescents that had $600 bikes and $200 uniforms, bike racks on trucks carrying 2 or 3 bikes, we arrived just as confident, but me with my K-mart bike, thick, red Nike sweatpants along with my stolen motorcycle helmet that I took from some dude that lived in my grandmother's neighborhood. Ok, now let's survey the magnitude of what I may have been feeling at the time. No, what I was really feeling! Considering the physical nature of the condition my bike was in and the distinct measure of the dress code in light of the others, it was lucent that I was a bit intimidated. However, egotistically in measure, my pride warranted the platform as if I was an ambitious myrmidon! I was like Michael Jordan on a quest for a championship!

I began to climb from Novice to intermediate and acquired a huge, glorious display of first and second place trophies from all around the tri-state area. My Pops had bought me a new $200 GT Racer bike and a uniform (gear racing) to go with it. I was nice! I forged

11

my way on to compete in many Grand Nationals and won 4 first and 2 second place finishes in each of them, receiving likes and interests from Pro teams such as, Action Wheels, Factory Racing, etc.

The thought of watching the ongoing parades of drug fiends skip up and down the block. My boys were buying RM 250 Quad Racer dirt bikes, Elite 250 scooters with systems on them, Jeeps, etc. This was very intriguing.

My cousin 'Mondo' was tall like me, skinny and lanky, and he was a brown skinned Keith Sweat looking dude. People used to say we looked like brothers, but till this day I still beg to differ. He was from Adam St. He introduced me to a whole new group of girls that all attended Magnolia Highschool. Mondo and I would chill at my crib and finesse the phone every day, calling damn near every girl that attended that high school. Mondo was getting money, hustling for this dude from Washington St., in the Germantown section of Philly named 'J-Doe'. So Mondo would sit in the house and count a few thousand dollars in front of me. He was one of those brothers that had an entrepreneurial spirit, was innovative and ambitious! If he was to transcend his energy into the corporate world instead of the underworld, I believe he would've been the next Warren Buffet or Carlos Slimm. He also had 2 siblings, a sister and a brother, who will be integrated into this narrative. Mando's parents weren't fortunate, but they made do with what they had, making a little seem like a lot. His mother and I were close. She had a super great heart and was as beautiful as a worthy summertime flower. Despite their socioeconomic situation, they still never fell to depression or sorrow. They kept their heads above water regardless of their flaws, shortcomings and institutional visits. My cousin was an arrogant type dude. Couldn't fight for shit, but he'll talk trash all day. I used to want to beat him up myself and take his money, but I would always think to myself, "This nigga is my family. How would that look?" Again, I was big for my age, and I had grown an ego and also a lack of respect for dudes. So I was looking for "Rec" (Physical Recreation). It was just a matter of who, what, when and where.

12

One day, Mondo introduced me to this girl named Deeasia. She was 5 foot 2, 120 lbs. with a voluptuous butt. She was a caramel skin complexion, very pretty, a bright white smile, had the voice of an opera singer, and she was immoderately book smart. She lived in North Woodbury. Her and I would indulge in lengthy conversations on the phone. I mean for hours! Half the time people would have to make an emergency break through on the phone.

Mondo and I would ride bikes to her house. He was forthright with her cousin Lina. She was ok, a little on the chunky side, but cute in the face, very smart in school and mature for her age. But she was no Deasia! Subjectively, I was in love with Deasia. When Mondo and I would go over her house, her and I would sneak off, because her mom and brother were always home. We would go right to the back of this school called Shady Lane Elementary. The first time we had sex, she demonstrated an equal amount of excitement as I did! The pants that she was wearing were hugging every curve on her body. It was a beautiful, warm day, about 73ø with a still, calm, natural air flow. You could hear the birds chirp as clear as a song that was sung out of love, knowing there were 2 beings about to create some sexual harmony. I stood in amazement as her undressing began to reveal her flesh and the mound of her vagina, obviously awaiting the presence of me to provide her and my young lust with all that we had spoken about over the phone. In the process of both of us undressing, she took notice of the size of me (as I bragged occultly at times) and her eyes widened as if they were a double mass of the sun. She started to act a bit concerned.

"All that...For real?" she inquired.

As we laid down, our eyes locked in a moment of pleasure and worry as I entered her. She was moist and tight. With every endearing stroke that I delivered, she moaned in pure bliss. As she reached the point of orgasm she screamed a cry of euphoria that I was forced to muffle with my right hand. Her sweet cries brought me to climax as well as I ejaculated inside of her.

While we dressed, she repeatedly asked, "Daryl, did you cum in me?"

13

When we were done and walking down the street, my 'Aunt Patti Ann' pulled up on us. "Boy, what you cuttin' school for? Get in!" She dropped Deeasia off at home and then drove me to my grandmother's.

I can recall my grandmother, who all the grandchildren called 'Gans', as a gorgeous woman, effulgent and afflatus with much wisdom. She was a God-fearing woman that loved everyone, no matter who they were or what they existed to be. She would always cook those meals that you wish would never end! Just about 5pm dinner would be ready at her and my grandfather's house. I know this, because I spent plenty of days frequenting the luxury of their blessed home. I can remember the musical tone of Channel 6 News always blaring through the speakers of the tv in the dining room. My grandfather was a cool, calm, humble patriarch. He would always lead in saying grace. Sometimes he would ask me to say it. Immediately following, he would ask how I was doing. Then my grandmother would give her wisdom, and my grandfather would give his. She would plead with me to utilize my potential and stay away from people that are unproductive and negative. But you know how that goes... We tell our loved ones what they want to hear while we're "keeping it real" with our boys. My grandmother also always plead for me to put God first, educate myself and treat women with the utmost respect.

However, in my quest in finding myself and who I wanted to be in the world, I was striving to make sense of being able to concentrate on school work. It was clearly the distractingly decorated environment that existed around me that made this so difficult. Again, many of my associates were now knee deep in the drug game and continued to climb in their attempts to take care of their families and buy the things in which only grown men with good paying jobs could afford. I can't front...It was all a bit too enticing. I was like a fish in the water. The drug game was like the fisherman, and my associates were like the bait. I caught myself wanting it all and seeing myself rising above the very associates that I was fly with. I bit the bait, and for the very first time I made up my mind to

14

partake in this new wave that blanketed the ghettos of the United States of Amerikkka!

*****

"Life is what happens to you while you're making other plans!"

-John Lennon

I began with an *indefesse* sense of ambition. On my way to school one day, I was walking with some of my associates. It was Fat-Joe from South Philly, big head Rakim, originally from Ohio (I was smashing his sister, Rameena, which would come to haunt me later), and this dude Lee, who was one of those lames that wanted everybody to like him. So yeah, he was a bandwagon rider on the low, but at the end of the day he was still our boy. We used to stop at "Carmen's" before school to buy candy, play Ms. Pacman and grope on the girls that dug us. In the middle of playing the videogame that I was about to beat the high score in, I called my boys over. "Yo, come here for a second so I can put y'all on some shit." I knew they probably thought I was going to make a joke or talk about sports as that was the typical me. I was calm and cool about what I was about to reveal and knew it would benefit not only myself, but all of us.

Fat-Joe nudged me and said, "What's up D?"

With one hand on the joy-stick of the game and one in the pocket of my denim blue Lee jeans. I pulled out a knot of money and said, "This what's up!"

Simultaneous of the same responses echoed from them all. "Oh shit! Where you get all that money?" Lee asked.

I was steadfast in my smile and answered, "It's more for us where this came from..." I will later explain to you guys exactly how I was officially introduced to the lifestyle that had captured my attention and started putting easy money in my young and hungry pockets.

15

At this point, I knew firsthand that this would change the course of my life as well as others around me. It was quite reassuring to me that I now could give myself a sense of identity that would not only fulfill the many voids of hollowness in my life, but also give me power and the means to control the things that I had no control over in the past! Watching old school gangster movies, tv shows and even just the norm of recording the do's and don't's of life really left me questioning the many intricate movements and meanings in the lifestyle that I was paying so close attention to. Waiting for the greater things that I was told patience and hard work provided didn't root within me. I was very avaricious and obstinate. Obviously, it was selfishly all about me.

If you want to know who someone is, listen to what he or she says! "For the abundance of the heart the mouth shall speaketh..." (Luke 6:15)

As fathers and mothers, we strive to stimulate our creativity by listening to wise expressed thoughts. Our attention gives them the respect for their own opinion, a respect that will last a lifetime. We in turn, must listen to our youth, or we'll be raising a generation of angry boys and girls. Following as well, they will carry this anger into all of their future relationships if they believe no one is listening to them. This consuming anger will surface as violence, introverting, perversion, and cause them to develop an outright self-destructive/criminal belief system. Their self-esteem and integrity will be destroyed due to them being muzzled most of their lives-bound and gagged, prisoners in a rigid shell of outrage and despair.

Recalling a day at home, my mother had me doing chores. My sister had me in one of those irritable moods, and my anger was beyond the point of a normal brother's frustration. See, we would fight and argue just like any other set of siblings, but this day she had me boiling to the point of bursting. I reserved the right of righteousanger. I Love my sis! LOL!

Anyway, there was a visitor that was occupying the basement, and I was highly interested in retrieving a vigorous sexual vacancy in her

16

villa! She was from North Woodbury. As a matter of fact, she lived directly across the street from Deeasia, over on Broad St. Gia was about 5'6, thick in all the right places, short haircut, light brown skin tone, pretty smile and sort of chesty to. We met after our high school played Woodbury in basketball.

As we watched tv, in our zone, we spoke about a number of things, from hip hop to just talking about people in general. Mind you, we shared this large, wide orange type seat that my mother had in the basement. To be honest, my intentions were *ultroneous* due to our last encounter with each other that led to a sexual rendezvous on my mother's washing machine, which happened to be the first time we engaged in sex. Vividly in my mind was a plot to have sex with her again, but the presence of my sister was haunting the moment of my plans. Trying to bribe her to go upstairs turned out to be a difficult task. If you knew my sister, you would understand why she is a lawyer today.

Renee was fully aware of what was going on, but having the presence of mind to know that her big brother was involved with a woman did not sit right with her conscience, due to her intrinsic value as a young lady. By the way, she was only 9 years old.

Calmly, in my deep baritone voice, which I obtained at an adolescent age, I asked my sister, "Sis, can you go upstairs?"

She replied just as calmly with pompous question, "What do you think Mommy will say about this?"

I was taken aback by her curvy response. I wasn't really surprised, because my sister was an outspoken, witty and observative child of God. However, this now made it even the more difficult to get the necessary private time I needed to tend to my lingering sexual desires. I knew what I had to do to bribe her. I was quite sure that money would be the catalyst of her departure. As Gia lay comfortably with her head on my chest, my lanky arms wrapped around her and one of her legs over the side of the chair, she raised her head to kiss me. With my sister still in view, yo can imagine the awkwardness of that kiss. In my psyche, registered a light of wrong

17

doing. My conscience dropped a heavy anchor, but my flesh yearned for Gia every waking moment.

I offered up $2 to my sister for her immediate departure from the basement, but to my surprise she turns the money down, which prompted me to raise the gesture to $5. Once again, she dismissed my attempt to bribe her with what I believed to be high prejudice.

After a half hour of not being able to get my rocks off, I walked Gia to the door. While my sister was cock-blocking Gia and I had devised a plan for her to come in through the back door so we could continue our lustful excursion. I knew that my mother, father and sister resigned to their bedrooms upstairs for the evening. I was cutting it close by trying to sneak around the way that I was, but I was always selfish and thought less about consequences in a funfilled moment. Knowing the level of my ability to scheme and plot, I thought it to be easy as to figure out with accuracy what my parents were doing at certain times, where they would be and when. The stairs to lead upstairs would squeak on the fourth step from the bottom. Also, approximately 7 feet from the steps, just shy of the entrance to the kitchen, the floor would squeak. Knowing this gave me an advantage when it came to be alert to anyone's arrival or an attempt to enter the basement.

Instructing Gia to hurry into my house through the back door, I pretended to feed the dog we had, all the while opening the gate to the back-yard to let her in. She looked at me with a sneaky grin and said, "Boy, you crazy..." What she had said about me being crazy was just a figure of speech to her, but low and behold, I may have just subconsciously demonstrated the future of my belief system and stagnant reasoning.

I then proceeded to rush her to the basement as I locked the backdoor. I can recall my little sister sitting on the living room couch, eyes glued to the tv. Wasting not a second of our time, Gia and I rushed back to the rear of the basement where the washer and dryer were along with the boiler and some bikes. I grabbed a quilt and quickly made a pallet on the hard floor. We stripped, then I laid her down on the pallet and excitingly mounted her womanly presence.

Unprotected, we started to engage in an event of youthful sexual prowess.

About 15 minutes into the enjoyment, I was interrupted by the unmistakable sounds of those squeaks. Now, my big head was telling me to put an end to this before I get caught, but my little head was saying keep going! Of course I listened to my little head and kept going. Reality really struck me when I heard the sound of someone entering the basement. That's when I pulled out and got up. We both hurried to get dressed. I was dressed faster, as boys have less to put on. She still had her bra and so forth to put on. Trying to think quickly, I unscrewed the lightbulb to the ceiling light then planted my foot firmly in front of the door to prevent the intruder from getting in.

Unable to gain entry, the voice of my mother coming from the other side of the door. "Boy! What are you doing back there?"

With a shaky voice I replied, "Nothin'...the door stuck, and the light went out." As I strived to make numerous attempts to direct Gia to a place where she could hide, which wasn't an easy feat with all of her thickness.

My mother was growing aggravated by the second. Finally, Gia was able to squeeze between the hot water heater and heating duct. Bursting in like she was the police, my mother smacked me in the head and looked at me as if saying, get out of my way. I moved out of her way and for the next 5 minutes I talked small talk with my mother, which was highly unusual of me as I was an introvert type of young man. I could tell that my mother was getting suspicious of me. So before her antennas went up more than they already were, I decided to retreat to the other room, praying to God she wouldn't catch Gia's ass back there!

Just minutes later, I heard the roar of my mother glaring in anger, "What the hell?!? Get your ass out! And don't come back either."

Gia sadly walked past me with a worried and afraid look on her face, but she cracked a slight smile as if to convey that she was turned on by the thrill of being caught.

"His conduct often brings him into conflict with society. The psychopath is driven by primitive desires and an exaggerated craving for excitement. In his self-centered search for pleasure, he ignores restrictions of his culture. The conscious is highly impulsive. He is a young-man for whom the moment is a segment of time detached from all others. His actions are unplanned and guided by his whims. The conscience is aggressive in his approach to the desires. He can commit the most appalling acts, yet view them without remorse. His conscious has a warped capacity for love. His emotional relationships, when or if they exist, are meager, fleeting and designed to satisfy his own desires. These last two traits, guiltlessness and lovelessness conspicuously mark the psychopath as different in time and growth."

-Unknown

*****

"Tell me what you pay attention to, and I will tell you who you are!"

-Jose Orteg V Gasset

On an October morning I awoke to the sounds of Power 99 Fm coming out of my radio, which I always kept on to help me sleep at night and wake me up in the morning. I was bothered from a lack of sleep, as I had snuck out the night before and didn't make it back in until the wee hours of the morning. This made rising out of bed an arduous process for sure.

After showering and grooming myself while listening to my Pops old school "Rose Royce" tape, I got dressed. I threw on a pair of burgundy Lee jeans, white Latega shirt with the burgundy gator as the logo, and my Adidas with the burgundy stripes, running concurrently with the burgundy fat laces. Last but not least, I threw on my black and red Lumber Jack bomber with the fake fur hood. I spent several minutes in the mirror, checking all points, like I was US customs, making sure my image was sharp enough to attract all the ladies.

As I was departing for school, I mentioned to my mother that my day would run into night, granted that I would attend practice then spend some time relaxing at Fat-Joes's crib. Normally my mother would okay my request to do as I see fit, but she was spooked by some deep-rooted intuition. Now using my hindsight, I can tell from her tone. She said, "No! I need you home..." A mother knows, but on this day, my mother being the gorgeous, loving, caring mother she has always been, she permitted me to go ahead on the quest that I had planned for the night.

As I was walking down Swedesboro Ave. to Broad St., I made a stop in Ms. Scordio's corner store. She was a Hispanic lady that was about 60 years old. I felt as though she was prejudice, but she was nice when she wanted to be. I bought some candy, really just fronting in case my mother had watched me leave. Dipping into the store, she wouldn't get suspicious as to why I made a left turn. Exiting left out of the store, I walked up a block then cut another left. Walking up another half a block, I turned right into the alleyway. When I got to the other end of the alley, I pulled out the keys to the black 85 Maxima that was parked in front of me. When I got in the car and started it up, the official sound of Eric B & Rakim's "Check out my melody" was blasting through the speakers. Pulling out of the alley was a task, because I never knew when I would run into my mother on her way to work, or even worse, the police.

The Maxima was tough! It was an all black 4-door joint, gold BBS rims, small wing on the trunk and plush leather interior with a Pioneer sound system in it that rung bells.

Pulling up to the side of Carmen's corner store, I hit the horn a few times to get Fat-Joe and this nice, young beauty Lanet's

21

attention. Lanet was originally from Chester, PA. She was 5 foot even, 120 lbs., and her weight was distributed into all the correct places. She was brown-skinned with chinky, hazel eyes, and she was big on my boy Bee. He was more like a brother to me. He was 5'10, 160 lbs. and black as an original crayon. Dude was only 17 years old, but with a ton of gray hair though. Everyone called him Black-Bee. He was a great dude!

I pulled up to the back of Paulsboro High with Fat-Joe in the passenger seat. I wasn't supposed to park on school grounds, because lacking the proper permit to do so could get you towed, but I did so anyway. Sitting in the car, we discussed what took place the prior night. He mentioned how crazy the atmosphere was...

*****

The night before, there was a house party in west Philly, on 56th and Cherry St. The ratio of women to men was an amazing 3 to 1, light skinned, dark-skinned, caramel, thick, skinny, chunky, short, medium, tall.. You name it, and this party had it. There was such a wide selection of beauty that I couldn't keep my focus on one female!

Fat-Joe, Lee and I attended this party in high fashion of course, and along with THE COST of everything we had on was a large .357 magnum snub-nose revolver with a black rubber handle and 5 hollow point bullets ready to escape from the reigns of my triggerfinger if need be, right on my hip. An associate of mine that was actually hosting the party ushered us through it, introducing us to some west Philly brothers as well as some sisters. The fellas and I did some politicking, all of sharing some common interests. We were all into criminal activities. We all planned on knocking one of these chicks off before the night was out, and a few of us were even looking to expand our network. See, one thing about being in the streets is, you always look for a way to further your criminal plans or empire. So, connections play a prominent part in the success of one who plays the streets. Perhaps these opportunities present themselves through many different avenues. One thing I knew was that these opportunities were to be seized if I wanted to grow in my criminality.

The brother who hosted the party gave my boys, Fat-Joe and Lee the green-light to help themselves to all the fruits of the party as he wrapped his arm around my shoulder and said to me over Run DMC's "Rock Box" song, "This shit jumpin', right?" I was in awe and almost in a state of narcosis from all the beautiful women that were there. I believe this was one of the solidifying factors in my life that confirmed my extreme love and interest in women.

Walking through that party, my presence demanded much attention, considering the fact that with the attire that I was rocking I could've graced the cover of GQ Magazine. Also helping was my being a light-caramel skin tone brother with an ego as big as the city of Philly! It didn't hurt either that the host of the party, who I will call 'Spank' was an official vet in the hood that repped as what I call a "Hoodocto", short for Hood octopus. A Hoodocto is an individual that keeps their hands in everything on the land that is beneficial to themselves and others. Spank was a big, heavyset, 300 lb. 6 foot 4 brother. He was wise as a serpent and humble as a dove. Mind you, I held reservations of his intentions, because our relationship in the streets was still fairly new. In prior conversations, we revealed a bit of our personalities to one another. I wasn't a heavy-hitter in the streets as of yet, or even close to it, however, he dug my style.

With the .357 on my waistline, knowing I was "O.A." (out of area), I was conscious in a nefarious way, ready to put a bullet or 2 in anybody who opposed a threat. I followed Spank through the house, and to my surprise, the house was connected to another house next door. Spank opened a door, leading us into a room that had one of those office chairs and a big screen projector tv and an Atari game, Caleco vision in it, a stereo and tapes that numbered in the hundreds. "Yo, you tryna get paid?" Spank asked me.

"Do you like women, cause to me it's a equal value?" I replied to what I took to be a rhetorical question.

I can't remember exactly what he said after that, but his explanation of how this money would materialize was very intriguing! He proposed that he had a fence for cars and he would give me 2 to $500 off each and every car I brought him. He went on to elaborate that there may be from 2 to 5 cars needed. We spoke for about a half hour before re-entering the party. Spank introduced me to a friend of his girl. I forgot her name, but I didn't forget that night! We danced slow and fast, grinded and humped. At 14 years of youth, you can imagine the type of hormones raging through my body. I recall this young lady and I making our way outside my car. She was shocked by me attaining the material essence before her at my age, and she was a little older than I was. If only she knew, this car was hot as fish grease! In the midst of my pseudo-intelligence and *paronomasia*, I knew I had her right where I wanted her in order to fulfill my sexual desires.

Despite how busy we are with women, when drama jumps off, all attention zero's in on whatever the issue may be, and something jumped off. My first thought was my boys. I was aware that Fat-Joe and Lee were a distance away, and I was wondering if they were in any danger. Despite the relationship one may have with a known factor in the hood, 2 things still existed. One: There are always dudes on the outside that will still try you, because you're not from their hood and their women are digging you...And two: that same known factor that you thought stamped your G-pass (ghetto pass) may work it on you...

Pushing the young lady to the side that I was with, I rushed over to the crowd, heart damn near beating out of my chest as I was a bit nervous. Shit, I had every right to be. I was in west Philly at 2 in the morning on a block that was just a shade away from being pitch black. Visibly clutching the .357 and calling for Fat-Joe and Lee, I got no response. I spotted Spank ahead of me, speaking with his hands, like people do when they're in a heated verbal dispute. As I got closer to this dispute, I realized that it was a physical fight, but one that was formulating. Then, in the blink of an eye, this dude snuck Spank. Spank ate the punch though and delivered a blow of his own. Literally out of nowhere, a mob of both males and females were brawling! Normally, the logical sense of reasoning would relay throughout the brain to retreat from amongst such a chaotic scene. I wish that I could admit to you that the once blessed words of my grandmother and father, "...stay away from people of no value..." and "...show me your friends and I'll show you who you are..." were dormant in my mind and heart, but that would be a lie.

With an impulsive, knee-jerk reaction, I raised the .357 and let off a shot over the heads of this crazed melee. Then, 2 more followed as everyone began to disperse. This I may admit stamped the notion that power presented itself in many forms. One form was "The power of The Pistol"! In amazement, as I escaped to the car, the pouring of an invigorating feeling dressed my inner-being, leaving my ego to rush more of what had just taken place. An internal monster was being born!

The female was already in the passenger seat awaiting my arrival with a look of slight fear hidden by a smirk of excitement. Seeing this only confirmed what I had bore witness to, not only in the streets, but in movies and books; that gangsters and bad-boys get the first in all, and good guys finish last.

Despite the positive role models that were a vivid factor in my life, I bought into the dream that the streets, either selling drugs, stickups, or fencing stolen cars would increase the popularity of my name and lift me beyond what I now can identify as my socio-economic situation. In my little psychopathic mind, I was right on line to reach the highest pinnacles possible:

"In this context, it becomes necessary to find the means to infuse the mind of young men with what is lost without discipline in a demanding situation. For the black young man, we must find ways to punctuate his psyche with commitment for family and race, community and nation, with motivation for responsibility, along with personal mastery."

-Amos Wilson

*****

25

I had seemed to lose control of my culture and my youthful socialization just as many black youths suffer from. Boys reach physical puberty readily enough; indeed, more precociously than our female counterparts. However, it is far more different and complex when it comes to advancing into the stage of social puberty. The young woman actually exceeds us in that stage of development, outdoing us in levels of maturity as pre-teens and teenagers.

We must recognize and actualize the difference between physical and social puberty in the Black boys' development, just as there is a difference between physical potency and social potency. Blocked from the avenues to political/social power and position, social potency, the black youth may too often feel impelled to over compensate in the physical--leading to fend for his very own decisions and direction. Sadly, this is where foolish pride, exorbitant egos, destructive decisions and unfavorable direction comes into play and our Black boys get inaugurated into a life of crime!

*****

Attending school happened to become a burdensome task, due to my new-found revelation of street economic empowerment! I had my share of ups and downs in class, attempting to pay attention long enough to learn the basics. It seemed frivolous to strive to excel in what leveled out to a zero to me at the time. I was losing the sense of value given to me by my grandparents and parents. Getting an education and doing the right thing like they always preached to me was starting to fade the black. However, still involved in the sports that were connected to the school and the assortment of girls that I had my pick of the litter with, ended up becoming a day camp for me. By night, I was attending the streets! Truthfully, I had to sneak out of my house to do majority of the things that I wanted to do outside of school, which I did quite frequently. It wasn't easy for me to sneak out though. The way my room was structured in the house, everyone had to travel through my room to get to the bathroom. The house only had one bathroom, and my room was the conduit. In case my mother of Pops got up to use the bathroom, I had to come up with a makeshift dummy to place in my bed in place of me sleeping. It was all good, because I always slept with my head under the covers anyway with the music on.

On numerous occasions, I took my mother's car or Pop's van to perform my criminal exertions. When I just wanted to cruise around, I would take my Pop's customized van, because he had a stereo system in it that was loud, like that of a symphony when it was turned up. I would feel an enormous amount of guilt at times when I would really think about my wrongful doings, knowing how much my mother and father strived to support me and teach me the essential elements of life. You know, having the right morals, principles and values. It was crazy, like half of me didn't seem to feel at ease with the things I was doing. I remember worrying not just about them finding out the many nights I was taking their cars, but also that I was committing mischievous acts in them. Nevertheless, my daring conscience still would seem to find its way around the guilt and fuel my self-fulfilling misbeliefs. I wonder if I really even loved my parents the way I proclaimed to have at this point?!?

CHAPTER II

A RISE OF ACTION!"

This night in particular that I am about to inscribe is that lifechanging introduction that I said I would detail for you guys. Things didn't feel right on this night. I was having one of those gut-feelings that you're not supposed to ignore, but in my impulsiveness, no moral gauge or standards were taken into consideration. I went against all intuition and proceeded in my quest anyway.

My mother was still up. She was in the kitchen doing last minute chores. Time was cutting close though, so I wasn't about to allow her being up to hinder me from my roguishness. The only way I could get out right then and there was out of my window, which was on the 2nd floor. I had to hang-jump from the window. I would hang from the window with one hand, shutting the window with the other, then jump down, landing on my feet in a 4 foot space in between my mother's car and the house.

The things we go through to escape being caught doing the wrong things in life is crazy when analyzed from the perspective of one who has grown and leveled up from such low stages in life! I had to literally push my mother's car out of the driveway and down the street before starting it up, so I wouldn't alert her with the unmistakable sound of her engine.

After getting the car started, I drove around to Adams St., where I stopped to pick up Lee. He was out on the block, getting to the money.

Adams St. was one of the main blocks in Paulsboro that produced a high level of drug activity, which meant lots of money was produced as well. On the middle of Adams was another street that lead to a section called "The Bottom". It was straight gutter down there! A block opposite of The Bottom was Washington St., another open-air drug market where 20's of powder cocaine were pushed every minute of the day and night. A connect named 'J-Doe' supplied everyone that stepped foot and hustled on Adams and Washington, and I would soon have my debut on his display of criminal plays.

Lee and I engaged in some small-talk over the sound of a tape I made when I was up north of the a popular up north radio station, DJ Alert. Arriving at our destination, in Woodbury, the atmosphere seemed to be so elaborate that I knew we would succeed in our endeavor. Parking in the back of Woodbury Manor Apartments, we ended up stealing 5 Pontiacs, 2 GMC Jimmy trucks and parked them all over the town!

In the midst of my criminal expose, it is shameful to say that I didn't have a speck of remorse for using my mother's car to perform these criminal acts, destruct property and deprive a company of its property. I wasn't aware of the fact that my actions may have been causing an economic crisis, increasing the taxes of the residents. I also disregarded the reality of only being 14 years of age, unlicensed and barely experienced operating a motor vehicle. Were our actions just plain suicidal? or did our age justify our foolishness?

Lee and I discussed driving back to Paulsboro to drop my mother's car off at my house, then back-tracking to pick up one of the sitting stolen cars. We then planned to head over to Philly to meet up with Spank. On the way, all I could see was money percolating in my head. Both Lee and I seemed to be comfortable enough with what we were doing to laugh, joke and smile in the midst of all the felonious things we were doing. When we pulled up to the 6th car, I got in the driver seat and went to start it up. To my astonishment, a Woodbury Police car was right behind me and activated the lights, signaling that I was busted! I immediately thought about how I could get out of this sticky situation. I first thought about how hurt my mother would be if she had to come visit me in yet another institution. Unfortunately, this thought hadn't come to mind until I was up shit's creek! I had the no surrender, no retreat embedded in my mindset before I left the crib. So my only option was to take chase! I took off and sped all through Woodbury, Deptford and West Deptford, then into Paulsboro with what seemed like the entire police force on my trail.

Nonetheless, it ended with my deployment from the vehicle in an area that I was familiar with. I ran on Thompson St. to the top of Swedesboro Ave. and into Lee's mother's house. She hid me there for about an hour or so. Then she drove me to my requested destination, where I paid her $50 for her assistance. In 1986, $50 was like $150 today.

I was able to retrieve one more car as brave or stupid as I actually was. Police were crawling throughout the stillness of the night in the quiet suburban town I was in. As selfish as I persisted to be for some money--laying my life upon the world--was not morally worth it at all.

After dropping off the last car, I was able to make it back to pick up my mother's car, drive back to Paulsboro, park it, and sneak back in the house through the dining room window. I was always greeted with energetic excitement by the massive German Sheppard we had, Spike.

I went down to the basement quietly to count the money that I had come up on as I came down from the adrenaline high that had enraptured throughout the course of my uninhibited night. However, another high came over me as the count continued to rise, $500...$1,000...$1,500...$2,000, and a total of $2,500 in just a night's work!

Jumping headfirst, I began to chase the illusions of a game that I was sooner than later to start losing at, creating an immoral vacuum in my family!

Instantly, plans of diving hands first before using my brains began to take place, and I wanted to put together a team that would support these illicit plans that infested my mind, heart and lost soul. I was transitioning into a life that my mother and father would never have approved of. They strived to blanket and equip me with the life as best known to them, but my mind was made up of these idealistic dreams of a sybaritic future. How was I to actually begin achieving these things under the roof of my law-abiding parents? In my subconscious mind, it was immoral and disrespectful to the both of them, as well as my little sister. I was an embarrassment to my entire family. Yet, I was not in a state of energetic moral compass.

School was not a cultivating mechanism for me at all, given the discovery of my subjective realities, what lay before me. Being very uncomfortable with school's curriculum, there was clearly an unequal value in my priorities. I hated doing the school thing at worst, and at best there was the presence of females who were the target of my interests. I knew arriving to school daily should have been and was supposed to be a focused effort to get an education in order to attain future successes, also to live out all the instructions that my parents reiterated all throughout my existence. What was I to do now?

*****

Lee met me in front of my locker intrigued about the pay that was placed in my hands after the night we stole all those cars. I informed him of his take on the come-up and also let him know that Spank wanted to do more business with us, but only if we could guarantee more vehicles within a specific time frame. I made known to Lee my plans to put together a team of us to get this done in a timely and professional fashion. Lee just shrugged his shoulders, looking a bit doubtful, but then went on to admit that the last time we went out he was quite *fastuous* of our chase and almost being boxed in by Woodbury Police. With my ambition to make things happen, I ended up convincing him to run with my plans.

I pulled a pound of currency out of my pocket, which was too much to even have in my pockets at school. I peeled off Lee's share from our ignominious criminal earnings. His eyes widened in awe. In the midst of our business, a female that was occupying the locker next to mine was nosey enough to see me flip through the bills and give a Tourette's-syndrome like outburst.

31

"Where you get all that money from?" she inquired.

I paid her no mind and handed Lee his $600, which he was extremely grateful to receive. I couldn't wait for the school day to finally come to an end, so I could find somewhere or something to spend my money on.

Lunch was a festival of goodies and a time for me to do my showing off. I bought donuts, cakes and pies for even people who weren't really digging me. I had a hidden agenda and purpose that would materialize in the near future though.

Not necessarily caring or considering the impact of my decisions, I was motivated by my own greed. I subconsciously indulged in my own destructive reality, ignoring my place in society. I now admit that I had no clue what life actually entailed. All that was ever said to me went in one ear and right out of the other. I did know right from wrong, however, adhering to what was right was an entire petition that my brain wasn't willing to process at the time. Seeing the condition of Black people and the way they struggled to live life so mediocrely the way my parents did was not a realistic means that I could understand. I watched my parents work faithfully, day in and day out, pay all their bills and be a great example as to what it means to exemplify the essence of a working class, married couple in an urban area. I wish I could openly admit that this made things easier when it came to following the rules, however, that is far from the truth of the matter.

*****

As the months passed I continued on with my criminal conquest to steal cars by the numbers. There wasn't a make or model of car at this point that I hadn't experienced driving. We even began to take random trips back to "Brick City" (Newark, NJ) to the port, where they stored brand new cars. These cars were straight from the dealers and fresh off the ships.

*****

When you spend time in state ran programs or prisons, your synopsis becomes "Criminology 101, 102 Universal". These were the sorts of topics of discussion that were had on a daily basis, drugdealing, fights, girls and rap music... Other than that, the system (federal and state institutions and programs) do not equip you with the proper articulate academic correction that is supposed to grant a man or woman a better quality of life. We need to be professionally helped from an authentic heart to make the quality of life better. Any state officials or individuals in position to make a change, take note of what I just stated in this paragraph.

*****

My mother was beginning to become suspicious of much of my activity in and out of the house. I was good at hiding not only my feelings, but what I would do in the dark shadows of my home life. Mom Dukes questioned me on a daily basis about my daily adventures. Low and behold, I was great at lying with a straight face to my mother and father.

Periodically, I felt as though I was an outsider, like an adopted kid that they stumbled upon in a friendship from someone they went to school with or something. In my head and heart, I was different. I didn't think like my mother, father, or sister. To me, I was from another planet with a sense of wanting to belong. Why couldn't I feel comfortable enough to speak openly with my parents? I don't know. To compensate with the way I felt and what (in my mind) society offered, I went after the things in life that I always wanted and thought I needed, the luxuries!

*****

On the weekends, Adams and Washington St. became not only a high siege drug market, but a natural Party City. There were popular spots out there, "The Wonder Bar" and "Loretta's" just to name a few, where patrons would come from areas as far as Delaware, Camden, Central Jersey, and of course Philly would come dressed to impress, cars on fleek and so forth.

On this specific night, it really was a *flagitious* idea for me to be on such a block considering the fact that I was only 14, and it was after midnight. The block was drug infested, parties were in motion, and I was in a stolen vehicle. Internally and externally, being in places like this seemed to make perfect sense to me for what I had seeded in the root of my interests though. I was introduced to an open world of what I thought to be congruous in the life of Black folks in the community. Social positioning began to subconsciously unlock these dark, mysterious wonders I had within.

My interests were so far removed from what existed at home. I had lost my identity. In hindsight, I wasn't studious enough as I was expected to be, like my more positive and affluent role models. I never clearly understood what it meant historically to be a Black man, nor did I respect the renaissance of my ancestors. Chief among me was my disdainful taste for anyone whom existed to be anything other than who "I" was. But who was I? Things were happening in life, but I never knew why, what, or even where...

This December night, I returned from sneaking around with Deasia. When I snuck out and drove to her house, I would park on a backstreet that was adjacent to her backdoor, in North Woodbury. This made it easier for both of us to enjoy our sexual escapades. Considering these were great measures of disobedience and a recipe for future harvested actions that were conducive to failure, I didn't care to think beyond the satisfaction of my adolescent lust.

Lee, Mando, M.E., Chuck, Teeman and a few others were standing in front of Mando's grandmother's house. Mind you, the whole block is packed with people inside and outside the bars. Women were everywhere, drug addicts were through and through, like a bank cashing checks. I greeted everyone as usual and engaged in small talk with the fellas. Mando had made a sell to a car full of Caucasian men for $200! On this block, back then, it was moving at the fastest pace. Processing all of what my *indefessed* mind resumed to record was relatively one of the greatest feelings I ever experienced! It was almost equivalent to my first time having sex! I knew I wanted in. So right then and there I requested through Lee for J-Doe to speak with me. LOL! I expected J-Doe to speak with me via my request. I was foolishly prideful and egotistical.

The fact in the matter is that, I never admired a person himself, because the heart has its own reasons, reasons in which it does not know. The subjective mind will cause the mouth to speak the abundance of its truth.

Now aware of this fact, it would only emerge when my pseudo intellectual acuteness pulled its triggers. Being that there lacked a presence of prudence and honesty, the under-society of the streets carves that neuro-pathway of its own expectations and cynical values.

J-Doe ended up asking me if I was capable of getting money while my Pop was working for County Corrections. Winning his confidence, we both agreed on a fair market value as far as my take off the proceeds from the drug-labor that I was about to be an employee of. I was going to be getting $30 off of every $100 pack...

*****

The holiday school break was arriving. My tireless efforts to be attentive were starting to evade my half-better judgment. Myself and a number of my cronies happened to be in a "special class". They weirdly called it the rubber room, which was by correct definition a class for special curricular interest to bring your grade level up in whatever class you were failing in. For me, it was math and science. Aside from the mentioned, I attended regular classes. For some guys, they had all "special classes". The rubber room was a circus! Now that I've stopped to think wisely, I'm apologetic to the 2 who ran this class, Ms. Cee and Ms. Vee. In class we were umbellic, remorseless and rowdy to say the least. I was a hyper, angry, impulsive, desultory youth coupled with the anchor of an insuperable ego. This made it impossible for me to even be taught! Furthermore, I held a slightly distasteful feeling toward these Caucasian people.

As educated as I stand before you today on history, race, politics, economics, etc., I was in total darkness then! The only history that frequented my conscience were depicting images of the movie "Roots" by: Alex Hailey. Other than that, it was what my friends would extend to me and what I had experienced myself with white people. I was fully aware that Caucasian people lived a much more pleasant and comfortable lifestyle than people in my community. I was very inquisitive as to the reasons why they exemplified much happier lives...They were much more peaceful, joyful and free-living with better jobs, homes and neighborhoods. Seeing this, along with an insightful view of life, knowing Black folks were marginalized would end up being the main factor for me continuing on with my *dissembling* ways. In retrospect, what we were going through wasn't just an epidemic. Our existence was a pandemic! I knew that not only I was different, but my entire race was different than the race that persisted to dominate us.

*****

One week before Christmas, I had not a single dollar in my pocket! Spank had gotten locked up for an attempted homicide and weapons possession a month prior. His associate remained on the run with the same charges. Although I was in tune with his associate, it was difficult to broker deals due to the lack of trust and familiarity.

J-Doe persisted to provide a number of fallacies, failing to come through the way he said he would and leaving my interest not in the new economic hustle, but in a fallacious sense of being. I was not at all gaining that social position that I had been seeking...

I began to lament over the fact that I was being pushed to the side-not respected as the intent of my nature sought out to be. Anger, frustration, resentment and embarrassment are all a result of such disdain the seed of dolosity befits to its structure. So it behooved me to act accordingly in order to earn respect, by taking what I wanted, and what I wanted was recognition. I was willing to do whatever it was that I had to do. I was trained to go!

In such axiomatic occurrences like the financial bind I was in, FatJoe would serve as my crutch. As problematic as it was, perhaps we were co-dependents in each other's bullshit! We fueled one another's egos by not checking the balances of one another's logic and reason-rights and wrongs. We would openly persist in any criminal spectacle that would serve our selfish needs, in total disregard for the best interest of our parents.

I never really considered the existence of the next day, or the next few years in light of plans, goals and endeavors. It was a clarion of a
"now" that was all about "me"! What was wanted, needed and desired was what I would acquire in my impulsiveness to satisfy "me"!

School was boring, far from amusing and beneficial. Home was a frantic search for some sort of *formosity" that didn't seem to be there. I continued to experience a brush of discomfort around my parents.

As I was sitting in my basement 3 days prior to Christmas, my mother called me to inform me that Deeasia was on the phone. While Deeasia and I engaged in conversation about minor issues, there was a sudden change in her tone as she admitted that she had to tell me something. Before I responded, she said, "I hope you won't leave me if I tell you this!"

My mind jumped straight to infidelity, thinking she may have cheated on me. "...I'll kill her!" I thought. Then my subconscious spoke to me. "...Even as she did cheat, wouldn't me wanting to kill her constitute a double standard and render me a hypocrite?!?" I slept with numerous other females throughout the entire duration of our relationship.

Deeasia was a great asset! I was just hoping her cheating wasn't the fact of the matter in this case. Then, it came out. "I'm pregnant! What are we going to do?"

A great part of me felt elated by the news, considering the level of love and interest I had for her. However, conscious of my own wrong doings with other females, the most imbecilic response blurted out of my mouth. "Are you sure it's mines?"

In reply to my idiotic questioning, she hit me back with a dial tone!

*****

Girls and the streets were calling me. Very much motivated by my own greed, I wanted nothing more than to acquire more money and have more fun!

I called Fat-Joe and told him I was coming around. As I grabbed my jacket and went to go exit the house, my mother asked where I was going. I told her I was going to Fat Joe's, and she immediately told me to do the dishes and feed the dog. I stated that I would do it when I got back, but that didn't work at all with Mom-Dukes! She just gave me that "MOTHER LOOK"! So I did as I was told.

In between time, Fat-Joe called wondering what was up with me. He said that Lee was over his crib and needed to talk to me. Sensing the urgency, I hurried up with my chores then rushed down the street and around the corner. It wasn't just Lee there, but also 5 females from around the hood. After greeting Fat Joe and Lee with handshakes, 3 of the 5 girls spoke. The other 2, I hated to the bone! Lord knows they hated me as well!

From the summer of '85 on to the next year, one of the girls that was there, Maya K, and I messed around on and off. Then I met her cousin, Margosia, who I had a fun-filled few nights with in my basement. It got back to Kaya, and I was hated by her from that day on. As for the second young lady, she was just riding with her friend.

Lee, Fat-Joe and I filed in to the kitchen table. Lee pressed on me that him, Mando and J-Doe stood on Washington St. and my name came up, inquiring about my ability in containing an economic position in the illicit drug trade. Right on the spot, the cells in my brain spun from the essence of *enantiodromia*, and I wanted to dive straight in.

It was not however so possible that my conscious mind could actually separate the good from the bad. People, places and things are very much an essential part of ones thinking and being. Slowly but surely human depravity harvests a more abundant garden of

38

lawless truths. There were no seeds of internal confidence at all to trust in the small amount of wisdom that lie pistil within me.

It is said that, "trust is the lubricant of society!" Nevertheless, the lack thereof remains a vacuum in our communities. And continuing to thread a weak fabric of values opposes to our historical authenticity displayed by our forefathers and ancestors.

The morals, principles and values of our parents and grandparents held in our communities were unambiguously dissipating and at rapid succession due in part to the systematic marginalization and muteness of Blacks and Hispanics. We then perpetuate this inward anger into an external marginalization of ourselves.

Home is supposed to be a place where anyone could or should feel content in what surrounds them, whether it be the presence of trials and tribulations, or the badinage that's supposed to exist to give a home its meaningful joy. Nevertheless, I was not too interested in the fabrics of this sort of comfort being that my actions dispelled these specific contingencies that I sold my soul to in the least; the streets and all that they entailed. If only I would've knew THE COST of just entertaining the seed of thoughts planted in my psyche. Because of this, I would end up staying in places longer than I was willing to stay and paying more than I was willing to pay. In retrospect, the wish to repudiate the decisions I made upon an optical sense laying at life's exposure sort of haunted my subconscious.

*****

A traditional Christmas eve is usually supposed to be spent at home with family in comfort. As the plot thickened within me, I sought to find my interests across town, where I anticipated joining the ranks of the very ones whose images I used to idealize. I felt like what they were doing was what life was all about. I was sadly mistaken though. I didn't have a clue as to if there was genuine love, respect or even a sense of safety there.

My environment was a decent structure considering all in scope of what was shaping around me--granted my people began to evolve into many roles of progression. Moreover, I still saw the worst in the community that I was residing in.

I took it upon myself to leave from the warmth of my home to chase a dream that held no promise nor warmth like that of the home I was blessed to have. Walking down Delaware St. in 20ø weather, thinking ahead and putting the cart before the horse, I already had the first $500 that I would make spent in my head. Before I could reach my destined area, a car pulled up on me and the driver side window came down. The voice of a female blurted out, "Yo...get in!" It was Angie, J-Doe and Lee.

What's the chances of this? It seems as though every time Satan has a plan for ones destruction, he always opens the floodgates for the avenue most traveled.

Choices... If I could only have offered a piece of reality and common knowledge to myself back then. If I could go back in time and talk to myself, I would've asked, "What's the difference between the life you're living and the life you want to live?"

I later found myself involved with an additional plight with people whom sought to use the means of my gifts, the strong love, loyalty and kinship that I was passionate about.

At J-Doe's home we spoke on what we expected from one another. Off of every $100 pack, I would pocket $30, and as I progressed there would be promotions and opportunities for me to make more money. This was the beginning of another feeling, purpose and need that I never felt back at home. I was chasing what I thought to be the answers to my questions that my inner belief systems demanded answers to as a teen. I was now officially a part of a faction that I felt would make my being concrete. It was really just the vision of others, how "cool" I could be and how tough I would prove myself to be.

CHAPTER III

"COGNITIVE DISSONANCE"

Back at home, my mother was preparing the atmosphere for a more fitting holiday spirit. I can admit that despite the dilapidated area we lived in my mother and father always attempted to structure peace in the thick of all the confusion. Regardless of what, things were not all good in our circumference. There were times that I wished to be made aware of a more in-depth understanding of why the many things that ignited my behavior would happen when I did things contrary to my parent's liking and not so much what I've done. In my household, if you did something that caused a person to be angered you were prone to either a fist, belt, pot or pan, slap, or at best just a verbal arsenal. Moreover, *vapulation* took precedence.

Christmas was always my favorite time of the year, alongside Thanksgiving and random barbeques. Family orientation has forever resonated in my heart and soul. The Cosby Show was actually my all-time favorite tv show, not only because the 80's lacked the presence of primetime positive Black tv shows, but I saw a house of success and happiness. I also saw a great sense of humanity that expedited the meaning that, "life is a great adventure or nothing at all," which is Biblical context of Abraham (the father of faith).

Besides the numinous presence of my grandparents that consistently seeded in me over the course of 14 years, there lie within me as well a seed of *nullibiety* that began to take root with every thought of my new street amenity. Considering such, I maintained the... Better yet, I tried to maintain who my family expected me to be when I was around them. Being self-disciplined should have grown in me from the seeds of all the positive manners that had been bestowed upon me--sober minded. For the Greek translation of "sober-minded" is "Sopron", which means a person that is about spiritual things and does not have the reputation of a clown. Some young people, like myself when I was younger, have a featherbrained mentality. However, the longer you serve the Creator, honor your parents and observe life for what it actually is as opposed to what it appears to be, the more you see through a more congruous perspective. Unfortunately, for so many years I did the total and exact opposite.

Whatever you tell a person, you better critically analyze what you're about to say before you utter a word, because if you say it you have to deliver it. They say honesty is the best policy. Your word is like your credit in life, and just like your credit, you don't want to ruin your word, because it is oh so hard to restore. Lying also shows a lack of character and an inability to face reality. I found it true that are better ways to manipulate a person or a situation without telling a lie.

I had reserved an open budget in mind relative to greater things in life and all that came with it, not factoring in the unforeseen nature that this voluntary regulation offered. Still it didn't matter. I was only thinking, "Get me to another dollar!"

*****

There were previous times when I would post up on Washington, blend in and finesse my way into the likes of those hustling. If I wasn't posted up there trying to be in the mix, I was somewhere with a female. This day right here would be my day of legitimacy though! The block was sort of quiet and a little chilly out, but the packs of drug fiends demanding to get high was loud and clear as usual. Mando was sitting on this lady named Ms. Tina's car with one foot propped up on the bumper. I always had this ground shaking walk that many people just had to look twice at, confident, arrogant and grown. This dude named 'Yoob' that was out there hated it! I approached Mando, and he slid off the car to greet me in royal fashion. We locked hands like it was an arm wrestling match and embraced each other.

"What up cuzzo?" I asked Mando. Yoob was standing next to Mando but got no love from me. He was hating on your boy, and I was well aware.

"Nothin' much. It's quaken out here!" mando exclaimed, meaning a lot of money was coming.

"Yo, where Doe at?" I inquired. I noticed this look on Yoob's face like he had to take a shit or something, but I dismissed it.

"He outta town," Mando replied.

"You was s'posed to been out here dude," Yoob said as if this negro was J-Doe's puppet or something, trying to tell me where I was supposed to be. Lee then pulled up and parked.

I wasn't really in any position to question or demand anything; but then again, the penetrating arrogance in me pushed the cause a little. Yoob was supposed to be J-Doe's lieutenant. Cars, clothes females, Yoob had it from his affiliation with J-Doe.

I wanted to do and say all types of foul things to this dude for talking to me as if I were a peasant of some sort, but I was on another mission. So I asked him if J-Doe gave him the pack for me that I was supposed to get. Then this clown had to nerve to tell me that my pockets would stay on empty if I couldn't follow directions.

Now, my interest in women was the cause of my lateness, thinking with my little head instead of my big one, but that was besides the point. I wanted what I wanted right then and there. It was all about me!!!

Yoob and I engage in a raw verbal battle! I was never one to back down from anyone--never! If you talk slick; I talk slicker! You get loud; I get louder! You want to fight; I fight harder! And you had to really beat me up over and over again if I lose, and if you proved that I couldn't beat you with the hands, I was going to get a gun!

I was a quiet young brother though, more of the humble, alert and attentive type. However, there was an eminently evil seed festering inside of me that began to grow by the day. You know, thinking back, I believe that the hate I was beginning to experience was actually total discomfort and dislike of what I began to succumb to in regard to the devil's playground. The streets is its own person. It

43

is also a life of its own that speaks direct to the psyche and hearts of the countless men, women, and children, lying and tricking them from its whispers and ideological reason. The streets is the devil's choice of construct, his playground.

Mando and Lee tried to calm me down, but in my mind I really wanted to go get the gun and put this dude in a dirt nap! Instead, I waited for the level of threat to decrease and spoke.

"My bad bro," I apologized, not really meaning it, but peacing it up for strategic purposes. I walked over to him and reached out to shake his hand. When our hands were about to meet, I cocked back and snuck him! To my surprise, he ate my punch! Blows were exchanged for a few seconds until we tripped over the fire hydrant. Then Lee and Mando broke us up.

Back at home, I knew I had things to do that were expected of me. My sister and I would be prone to share specific chores around the house. Life wasn't all laying around and waiting for things to appear before me. We basically had inhouse jobs throughout the days, nights and years. I despised doing chores to the max! FOR REAL!!! In my head, why was it that kids had to clean up after adults. We have to do dishes, polish those long, heavy wooden coffee tables in the living room that came with the two wooden end tables (if you are old enough to remember), vacuum, scrub everything in the bathroom, iron moms and pops shirts, wash their cars, and the list went on. I'm thinking like, "Yo, I don't even drive y'all cars...Why I'm washin' the dirt off 'em?" However, later on in life I discovered the great parenting in what my parents put me through. When I was finally fortunate enough in life to lease my own dwelling, you would swear on your life that a woman dwelled with me by how clean and tidy I kept my spot. So I was being groomed into independence without being aware of the lesson until I was tested. I was given assignments as a youth so repetitively that great conduct was being internalized, but I didn't start seeing the right in their ways of treating me until much later than this.

We were lucky enough to have the first Nintendo. When we got it, all I wanted to do was sit around and play the game, lay up in my room and talk on the phone with females. I really just snuck around and did whatever I thought was amusing. More important, we would end up at my grandparents' house in Deptford, NJ. When they migrated there from Philly, my grandfather built such a peaceful structure of a home with his bare hands. the house was wonderfully small in size, about maybe 800 sq. ft., 3 bedrooms and a basement. It was such a warm, inviting, loving and spiritual home! Posted up in the left of the 4 corner room was the Christmas tree decorated with beautiful arrangements. Even ornaments that I made for my grandparents when I was a little boy still hung proud. Artwork that was created by the hands of all their grandchildren also embellished the long shelves that ran across the entirety of the walls. Even the lovely photos of, not only my mother, but my uncles and aunts in footies when they were babies still hung respectfully in the staircase to the second floor. The aroma of the best southern soul food you could ever tasted was a graceful presence throughout their home. Just visiting this wonderful home, you would probably beg to become a permanent resident of the 'Spencers'!

Considering the sounds of what I just mentioned above, how could I not digest the essence of this imponderable love?!? How impeding of my own growth, I was!!!

On most occasions there was usually the total fulfillment of joy, peace and happiness in the occurrence of my grandparents. Again, especially on Christmas! However, my joy would temporarily be implicit considering my conscious activity in the streets with no approval from my grandparents or anyone in my family for that matter.

It was readily difficult to maintain eye to eye contact in part of the heavy amount that lie within me. I was now complicit in things that were contrary to the Divine Creativity in the Bibles Genesis chapter two.

I believe it is when we start life out as a totally dependent child-when our needs for reliable safety and love to survive emotionally aren't met--that we send our bright, trusting and delightful child spirit underground to lock away for self-protection.

In a book I read called, Recovery of Your Inner Child by: Lucia Capacchione, she said, "...but the inner child never grows up and never goes away. It remains buried alive, waiting to be set free..." Therefore, when the ones we love in our lives can't be counted on for the amount of emotional attention and direction that is needed a part of our development gets stagnated and placed on hold. Also, our willingness to trust people, be open, spontaneous and loving goes into hiding. Walls are stacked around our inner child to assure that no one hurts us. Walls of toughness and defiance, all to protect that inner-being to seek that which appeases the inner rooting seed by any means. Hurt fertilizes bitterness, making it grow like a weed. Indeed, bitterness is like a root that sinks deep into the soil of our heart and spirit. When watered with resentment and anger, it springs up and causes trouble, defiling many around.

*****

US minorities have been part of a generation that historically in his or her image continue to cultivate wholeness by way of unified love in a community. The one thing that keeps Blacks and Hispanics on a treadmill, stagnating our progress is the preponderance of the root in our authentic hearts of   generalization that hopes to perpetuate communal acts of example in the face of White Amerikkka. However, in most situations in which people feel some sense of deprivation, it is due to the total difference in Black communities in contrast with the predominantly white communities. Not only before me was there the reality that I was different than my own family, but Blacks were completely different when presented with chances to exercise their own linguistics. In light, even towards my own, I noticed treatment of disparity, whether family, friend or neighbor. I wasn't fortunate enough back then to be in receipt of a clear understanding of the Why's... Okay, that is the problem. Now, what is the solution?

From comparing and contrasting "why" and "what", I find that "why" is the most imperative, significant and effective word to analyze and embrace. The Webster's Dictionary defines the word "why" as follow: "1. The purpose, reason, or cause for which..."

The main focal point may clearly eradicate the seed of "what" may grow from its roots. For example: If we were to focus on "what", which is defined as, which thing or which particular one of many kind, character, or designation, this would be the image of something formed from a purpose, right? Now, if an action arises from a negative seed and the focal point of the one witnessing this stresses and oppresses this "what", it then suppresses the opportunity to doctor, mentor and give precedents to the "Why".

It is to my fact that focusing on the good in a person negates the assumption of the bad. In positive psychology this articulates the presumptions of what is called the "Aristotelian approach" to human nature and development. This includes the view of the good person-the idea of the individual with a positive character, strengths, and given virtues.

Nevertheless, my outlook from within my life wasn't with an equivalent prospective as our white counterparts. My mother, father/family and others in the black communities had to work at a continuous pace, not to get ahead, but just to make ends meet and stay afloat.

There wasn't much of a presence of in-depth instructions as to what was really going on intrinsically as opposed to externally. All I knew was that life was a "hand-me-down" from the leftovers of the world, and comfort was not the reality of the Black communities' situation.

Although there was a home for me, despite the lack of, love was not enough of a force to keep me grounded. I had bonded with those whom proved to be like-minded and shared similar plans, strategies and goals (so to speak). Unbeknownst, I saw nothing but fame and fortune in the streets, which in turn blinded me to the downsides of the streets and the more positive role models that I had in my life, like my mother, father and grandparents. I unintelligently chose to live an illustrious life of crime.

I loved the presence of my parents so much, but I can recall times when there were specs of impassivity at home and in the streets. The intrinsic guilt of my hidden behaviors were an impeding factor, accumulating extensive cover-ups.

Back at home, I began to get extremely agitated by the amount of demands that were coming from my father. I told y'all that he was a disciplinarian, as well as a student/teacher of logic, grammar, rhetoric, etc. However, I failed to mark his astronomical efforts the he put forth to assist me in my stages of growth and development.

My life at this point was in its malevolent stage of this downward *prospicience*. Deasia, who was pregnant with my child at the time, was just about 2 months removed from the egregious process of an abortion. School had become out of my scope of realistic capability. I knew that there was more to life than just what I bore witness Blacks living as opposed to whites. I was going to find my own quick and easy way out!

*****

On a day that I was washing my pop's van, Lee pulled up with an unknown female driving. Even though it was February, it was a fairly nice day. We spoke privately about engaging in getting money. He stated that he copped his own weight aside from what he was moving for J-Doe. As arrogant as I was, I quickly began to curse JDoe, having reservations in my mind to stick him up all in part of him shunning me like I was some sort of peasant or something!

Similar to what Robert Greene said in The 48 Laws of Power, "...Patience will protect you from making moronic blunders. Like mastering your emotions, patience is a skill--it does not come naturally. But nothing about power is natural; power is more godlike than anything in the world! And patience is the supreme virtue of God..." Not seeing this fact of life would end up costing me and my family unimagined heartbreak, frustration and pain in future lenses.

Instantly, I pushed right into the drug game. I was making $30 off every $100 pack of cocaine I sold. Back in the 87, the fair market price for each bag of coke sold was $20. I was given a pack (a bundle of bags) that contained $500 worth of coke. So my residual would be $150, giving him back $350. Perhaps this was an agreement that seemed like a miscalculated equity. This of course was not a thought to consider granted that, against my better logic the illusion of THE COST of my economically interested behaviors were very much malleable upon me.

I was thinking I would just step right on the block and pitch a few bags of cocaine, acquire a heavy presence of pocket money quickly and retreat home. Well, that was one of my first illusions of the game. My first day in this strange world that I forged my occurrence onto. After serving about 6 customers my product, the next sell happened to be the very test of my capabilities and credibility.

A blue pick-up truck pulled up onto the side street that we called The Bottom. A slim Black man had gotten out of the truck and yelled, "I need six for a hundred!"

I responded promptly, but I didn't actually give him what he asked for. I only gave him 5 bags. The customer and I traded words as this dude tried to haggle me. I could tell he was getting agitated from my sarcasm. I mean he was a crack-head, a fiend, a junky that didn't respect his own self. So I felt like, why should I respect him? When I told him to get the f**k out of her if he wasn't copping, he humbly agreed to take the 5 bags. Little did I know, he had a trick up his sleeve! As I extended my hand to give him the 5 bags, he snatched the bags and hauled ass! I chased after him as he ran through The Bottom trying to escape me. I caught up to him and clipped his feet from behind, causing him to tumble over, but he didn't let go of those bags. I punched and kicked him a few times until he let the bags go and they fell on the ground. I picked them up and spit on him twice as I was walking away. When I got back to my post, I met by the laughs, jokes and hustlers 101 advice from the other hustlers that were out, 2 of which that weren't well liked by me. Deep within me, I reserved a right to commit some sort of physical harm upon them by any means, whatever my impulsive mind projected.

Amidst this new journey of self-seeking objectivity, was a semiconscience of selective human decency in the way that I conducted myself, treated people and responded to things. I guess you can say I was passive aggressive. However, the fear of missing out or being mistreated far outweighed the essence of doing good.

The wisdom of real life continued to be stagnant within, leaving me obtuse to such a change in sustaining truth. As a young man trying to find an identity by any means and being trapped in an image that the silence of my soul forged or began to forge a ton of bricks and mortar, sealing my social intellectual growth. For many years, I was blinded to this detrimental psychological growth.

In the community, if in fact you are not seen as equal to (or tougher than) those who are managing the streets, then you are a sheep in wolves' territory, waiting for slaughter. As a young boy, who wants to walk around with such a label or target on their back? I know I didn't...

Us males, our masculinity is exposed through the geographical and social construct in which we claim likes to such a thing that really has no authentic seed in us as Black Kings and Queens.

It is long understood that social recognition promotes healthy development, while being unseen and unheard threatens thriving. I felt as though it was healthier for me to assimilate to this culture that was a self-saving interest and would build up a reputation for who and what I wanted to be... Or better expressed, who and what I did not want, need or desire to be!

My criminal expeditions continued in their worst. The challenges that came from the wolves that resided in different packs, I was taking head on, and I wasn't backing down from anybody! My attitude and hate began to grow more in nature and my hunger for women was also beginning to oust from within. This would become a tangled web that I would have to weave.

50

Deasia and myself had departed after her mother forced her to abort our child. This damsel named 'Ganeen' was now my steady girlfriend. Deasia and I still talked, and I found myself just using her for sex. There was an absence of respect for her. I had acquired another sex partner named 'Cinda'. She was a junior at Woodbury High, and she was nice! She was 5'10, about 135 lbs, caramel complexion. As a matter of fact, she resembled 'Pepa' from the rap group Salt & Pepa. She had a job at Wendy's after school, and she had a great personality. There were a few girls from Deptford, Glassboro, Vineland, Camden and of course Philly that I had on my roster as well.

Sex became a release for me. There was really a list of plausible reasons for my treatment of my own perceptions of goodness and worth. This became another notch of recognition that served its purpose. I felt like I may have been on the brink of ostracism and there wouldn't be any benefit to what my internal self was striving to accomplish. In school I was not open to learning a damn thing! My closed mind made it easier to perpetuate this child-like search for meaning in life and position in the streets.

One thing that the streets have in common with mainstream society is that and individual's success depends on his or her ability to communicate and forge beneficial relationships with the right people. It's all about who you know and who knows you, but when neither is present, you have to be willing to take what you want or feel as though you deserve. I was prepared to do so by any means necessary!

*****

One night, I snuck out to hustle off the coke that I had in which lee gave me to get off. That night Yoob and I fought again. I ended up throwing him in a sleeper hold and putting him out. Shortly after J-Doe pulled up to speak with Fat-Joe and a few others. When he noticed I was out there moving, he asked if he gave me coke to sell. I told him no, and he told me I couldn't hustle out there. Immediately my ego and pride kicked in, because I was not the one to be ordered around by anybody, and everyone witnessed his attempt to punk me. But wait... I recall in our initial conversation JDoe saying I was a part of the family. So how could this dude front on me like this? This is what I thought to myself.

In my stance was a physical response of not moving. We exchanged words, curses and threats. Then Doe tried to swing on me but missed. I can't front, back then, Doe was big as hell. Remember, he was a damn near 300 lbs, 6'2, big ugly dude. In my attempt to fight him, he ate my punches and scooped me, slamming me on the concrete. When I bounced back up, the first thought that infected my mind was, "I'mma shoot you!"

This had put a strain on my novice drug career and those who were related to or in cahoots with Doe were giving me crazy looks in school and out. Mando began to call me 'Lip', due in part to my loose verbal attacks on whoever. The name also fit because of my big lips.
(lol!)

I would say whatever negatives were in my verbal arsenal at the time of delivery with intentions on piercing my attackers mind, heart and soul in a foul way! As humble as I was, I became disrespectful, unfiltered and bestrewed to a lot of dudes.

My step-father would say, "Show me your friends and I'll tell you who you are, then I can judge where you'll be in years to come!" I never realized the significance in those prophetic words of wisdom until the latter half of my life. 2 Timothy (3:2) says, "People will be lovers of themselves, lovers of money, boastful, proud, abusive, disobedient to their parents, ungrateful, unholy..." And contrary to the betterment of my real true self, I participated in the above. I was not aware that people, places and things had such a powerful effect on our belief systems, emotions and life's latter half!

*****

March of 1987, the consistency of my criminal behavior enraged to its peek after I received a phone call from a person that I had not heard from in months. In all truth, I should have just hung up, but my moral compass was not at work. This reconnection would be one of the determining factors that twisted my life even more!

Myself and my female acquaintance, Cinnda, sat closely on the enclosed porch, talking, hugging and kissing, just enjoying each other's vibes. My mother made her presence felt at the door, letting me know that I had a phone call. Cinnda gave me a look that said, "That better not be another girl", because my reputation was not one of faithfulness and monogamy. However, on the other end, the call from a voice that I wasn't quite familiar with at first.

"Hello," I said into the phone.

"What up yo?" the voice exclaimed.

"Who is this?" I questioned sharply.

"Spank!"

We spoke briefly of his current situation and then moved on towards my present encounters. You know, filling him in on what had been going on in my life in between the time of us not speaking to each other. I let him know that his boys wouldn't buy any-more cars from me since he was gone. He elaborated on why this was. Following his explanation, he made an inquiry.

"Yo, you ready to get this money?"

Again, my moral compass should have impulsively spoke to me. Instead, my impulsiveness imputed to more immoralities of life, and I told him I would be back in Philly as soon as possible! His reply was to meet him in Center City at The Galler mall, in the food court.

I would imagine from time to time how I felt every time I looked in the mirror. What I saw staring back at me would usually be a stilled face, confused looking with disdainful eyes. Before long, at times I could represent a specific favorable type of person or title, however, when a mirroring face of mine reflected back disdain and (or) was stilled, it created no reflection at all. That inner self-doubt would arise and cut into my self-esteem. I've learned now that perceived relational value increases when people feel accepted by others and decreases when people do not.

W.E.B Dubois in The Souls of Black Folk said, "It is a peculiar sensation...of always looking at one's self through the eyes of other, of measuring one's soul by the tape of a world that looks on in amused contempt and pity." Unbeknownst to me, I was being totally controlled by the same people that I sought to gain social recognition from. I wanted them to like me, to respect me and the man that I was becoming (so to speak). Where did I go wrong in my thought process and my decision making? How did I succumb to this hate with these disdained eyes and still-faced reflection? This wasn't what God created and what my mother birthed....

That evening, after I spoke to Spank, I asked my mother for $5, because my pockets were on lean! I had 2 punk dollars to my name! I walked to Romee's Record Shop on Delaware St. They sold a vast collection of drug paraphernalia from empty's (baggies to bag up drugs with. In my case, cocaine...) and scales to cutting agents. He was familiar with my face, because I spent a lot of money in his store buying tapes and records. Romee always knew me as a decent, respectful young boy in the hood. He also had a report with my pops. When I approached the counter, he met me with an inquisitive look as I requested to by a bottle of Bolivian Rock and a pack of empty's. Bolivian Rock is a cutting agent that is used in the production of cocaine to add quantity, depending on its level of purity. It's also used in process of cooking cocaine in to crack rocks. Legally, the empties are used for the preservation of coins, stamps and things of that nature. We were shown how to make universal use of such a thing in the drug trade. This way of packaging was first coined by the old school "Gangster" turned rat Nicholas "Nicky" Barnes, in Harlem, New York.

Expeditiously, I packaged the Bolivian Rock into the empties for sale. There's 50 baggies in a pack of empties, and there was enough Bolivian in the bottle to bag up thirty .2 of a gram sized baggies. They went for $20 each, equaling $600. Profiting from the sale of this would be easy in my twisted psyche, because although the cut didn't get you high, it looked like coke and numbed your nose or tongue, just like coke did. The majority of the people who bought coke off me went about doing the cocaine through their nasal passage.

What I was about to do was very dangerous! Selling beat bags could really get you in a world full of trouble, because people spent their hard-earned money to fix a chemical dependency that their body craved enormously! Some women would even "trick" (sell their bodies), indoors or outside for as low as a half of a bag, which is totally degrading and shameful, but there is no shame in their game! Men would steal from their own family members, children and friends to acquire money to buy these drugs. Therefore, selling one of these people something that wasn't going to fix their problem would surely create problems! I didn't see this far at the time though. Longevity was not engraved in my thinking process as of yet. Again, I pushed my morals, logic and common sense to the side instead of ahead of the mess I was creating that could possibly cost me my life in the streets!

The first 6 bags sold easy, within the first 10 minutes of me being on the block. Half of the customers were familiar with me already. So this made the task much easier. Because of my inharmonious occurrence with Doe, watching my back became a first instinct for me. Between Doe's cronies and the police, I was always on high alert. I also had stick-up kids and the customers that I was selling fake cocaine to worry about.

While managing the block that night, I went to the back of one of the trap-houses on the block to snatch up a few bags that I had stashed in a patch of grassy dirt I constructed that held my fraudulent cocaine, because I saw a customer coming down the street and I wanted to beat the other hustlers to him. When I noticed that it was a dude that I had already served. I dipped into the trap house, so he wouldn't see me. I knew what I was doing was wrong, but on my greedy and selfish agenda, I had to get it by any means necessary, so I could get enough money up to buy my own weight.

I heard a bunch of chaos and cursing coming from outside, so in defense of everyone that was out there, I manned up and went back out to face the confrontation from the customer who was beefing about the product. When the customer and I got in close proximity of each other, he started to point his finger in my face. He didn't just point, but actually made contact with my face.

"Motherf***er! You sold me some fake s**t!" he roared, in anger.

I ended up beating this dude up. In my mind, the fiend's filthy hands could have been anywhere! Plus, I was somebody! Who did he think I was? I hit him with a two piece. It didn't knock him out, but he stumbled backwards. As he was going down, I whipped out my .357 handgun. Before that, everyone was cheering and hollering, like it was a Mike Tyson fight or something. When the gun came out, everyone hushed as if a switch got turned off. The guy froze in instant fear.

"Ni**a, I'll blow ya' head off!" I threatened as I walked up on him. The closer I got, the more this guy balled up, like balling up would stop these bullets from hitting him if I decided to shoot. I was angry and the inner-devil in me wanted to shoot him, but instead I just struck him twice with the pistol. I can remember a bunch of blood trickling down his face, but what was more noticeable was a still voice, not just in the back of my mind, but literally in the back of me. These two voices were telling me,

"Shoot him in his big a** head...Kill that pu**y..."

As the guy cowered in pain, I told him to get up and get off the block. I kicked him in his behind as he parted and yelled obscenities at him. I had to clean this guy's blood off my gun from the water spout on the side of the trap-house.

"Yo, who was telling me to kill that dude?" I asked everyone that was on the block, but they swore to it that no one said anything to me. To this very day, I swear I heard someone's voice behind me, edging me on to shoot that joker. However, it could have been me being infested by the demons, who began taking over the internal residence of my own mind, body and soul! In any regard, after this pretentious incident, I retreated to the home of my mother and father.

CHAPTER IV
"UNBALANCED RECOGNITION!"

The Oxford Dictionary defines the word stigma as, "A mark or sign of disgrace or credit." In my quest/journey of self-discovery, I began to deem my actions as perpetuated by the "street credit" from peers that traveled the very dark road I was traveling myself. Assistant Professor of Pastoral Care and counseling at Condler School of Theology, at Emery University, Gregory C. Ellison II, author of Cut Dead but Still Alive wrote, "Though a person may receive some form of social credit from being stigmatized, stigmas are largely viewed as unjust signifiers of a person's group's character and identity. That, more often than not, stigmatized people are viewed as 'flawed', compromised, and somehow less than fully human."

The next morning, I arose from a night that excited me, and I knew what I had done impressed and excited dudes that were in attendance. I was betting on the fact that my actions would spread throughout the town. I thought about this and my meeting with Spank while ironing my clothes. Image is everything! So I made sure my PePe jeans and Latega shirt were pressed. I even wiped down my burgundy and white shell-toe Adidas with a toothbrush. I also brushed down my Lumber jack. I was more concerned with my outer appearance and what people thought than what my inner appearance was communicating to the world.

I left school right after my lunch period, leaving Fat-Joe at Carmen's. He was aware of my situation, and said he wanted in if anything were to jump off. I had a stolen Cadillac Fleetwood parked in The Manor, so I was good. I had money in my pocket, fresh gear on and a clean, white Cadillac. You couldn't tell me I wasn't that dude, but my ego would enlarge as this was only the beginning of my end. Despite the fact that everything that I had acquired was through these novel ideas that were consigned to the "new me", I was very much coming into visibility.

Spank and I spoke on what we expected to see materialize from the people, places and things around us. He was a fast talker, very slick with his words. Somehow, I was convinced by him to steal a certain amount of cars and he would hit me with a lump sum weekly. This, to me seemed like some real 9 to 5 work with a check and benefits. So of course, I declined as instant gratification had become a part of me. We ended up agreeing on $500 a car. We didn't shake on it. We both just accepted each other's word as bond. But in the life of crime, "there is no honor amongst thieves!" For some reason, trusting Spank wasn't in question though.

Back in Somerset Hills School, we occupied the same room for just about 2 years and became a bond of brothers. We fought together, jumped numerous of dudes, shared each other's clothes, and played on the same teams in sports. Long before my later initiation into the Bloods streets gang, the seed of "never abandon your brother" was already planted. We both, sometimes together, experienced racism firsthand. White people would call us "monkeys", "niggers", or "you people". Therefore, there was much more commonality than what may have appeared to one's eye. Us and others had grown a hatred for white folks, because of this imbalance of humanity and racial respect. I can honestly impute the fact that I was sure we were the object of stigmatic ridicule.

Back at home, my parents began to recognize and realize the slight changes in my behavior. I thought that I was inconspicuous enough to hide my faults and destructive ways, but a fact of life is that parents are the extension of God's creative conscience, and children cannot get from under the scope of reality. I'd developed sociopathic principles that were subconscious to my initial intentions and or purposes. But a parent knows the child that they've birthed and raised, sometimes better than they know themselves. The traits of a child are endogenously patrilineal and matrilineal versus external nature. The intimacy that begins during a mother's 9 month cycle does not end when the child is born and raised. Our mothers will forever know us better than we will know ourselves. have you ever heard the saying "A parent knows best"? This is because parents either have extreme experience and wisdom, seeing in us what they've already seen and lived, or they just have that intuition. Therefore, there were rapid question and concerns that spilled from my mother's heart and lips at me. i would just try my hardest to evade all of her concerns.

I started out on a ruptured and unfavorable identity with, surroundings and of course myself. I was practically below the standard of what it meant to be a Black young man, not really living up to my true potential and not fully paying attention to the conditions of society.

I became stuck in this trapping and execution of committed behavior, hence my latent cognitivity failed my true rite of passage that is based in historical African or Biblical customs, rituals and ceremonies. My Brother from another mother K-Bang* wrote in his spoken word Who Am I??? (Part 1): "I am a prestigious African American King, and I reign Supreme in every setting that I find myself in... Because that is just who I am..."

I will not elude from the fact that these females that I had begun to entangle in my web of lies, manipulation and deceit, were very good ladies. Not only in character, but also in school in other areas in life.

In the midst of my relationship with 2 of my females, Tawanda and Ganeen, they found out about each other and started arguing, bickering and fist-fighting almost every time they seen each other. I'm ashamed now to say, but back then having women fight over me was amusing and very influencing to my already immense ego. Having women fight over you was considered trophies on your ego. I picked Tawanda up from school and we rode to Philly to hit a few boutiques on South St. We went from there to The Gallery, then to Fairmount Park to relax. You know talking, doing a little cuddling and kissing. In my attempt to unbutton her pants to ease my hand into the front of her panties, she quickly gripped my hand and pulled it away.

"No! Not here..."

As persistent as I was, these attempts to meet my sexual desires would continue to fail. Tawanda was not an average girl, not like one of the usual's that I can easily dominate and manipulate. Nah! She was a bit wiser than I! During our time at the park, she began to ask a number of specific question, attempting to pick my brain and figure out my intentions. I have to remain honest, I wasn't even prepared for that line of questioning. It came as a curve-ball to me as majority of my women were just doing as I say and please.

"What do you want to be when you get older?" she asked, throwing me off guard. They kept coming too! "What do you want to major in when you go to college?" Then, the next question really threw me for a loop. "How old do you want to be when you get married?". Of course she hit me with, "Where do you see yourself in 30 years?" I'm like, for God sake woman! I was sitting in her Nissan 300z with a complete elementary frame of mind. How could I ever realistically measure up to the questions that she proposed to me? This, by far was the very first woman (advanced in her conscious) to send my psyche into a mobilized trek of self-fulfillment, and I questioned myself, the inquisitive character that began to originate! To my point, life was throwing me fast-balls and I only possessed the tiny fraction of life's skills to manage good hits!

*****

For many months to come, I proceeded in the same destructive and self-oppressive behaviors. I was putting forth less and less attention to sports, something that could've been my true passion in life. All of my true inner passions, that inner-child was dying, and a foolish man was being born! I was great in domestic capacities. I mean, at my age, I could cook, clean, wash my own clothes, and I was also learning how to fix things around the house under the tutelage of my step-father/pops. I always hated doing most of the things I was forced to do, because I thought that the things I was doing were things that women were supposed to do. Yeah, I apologize women, but I was a little screwed up in the head then! I would've rather had been outside getting into mischief or at best, just relaxing.

Still, I chased the streets and the credibility that came with putting work in in the streets. My grades were slipping drastically! It seemed as if everything in my life that had the slightest spark of positivity was on a downward spiral due to the *acrasia* that I had fell victim to. I continued to lie to my mother, negating all of her approaches that came from that mother's intuition that I spoke about previously. My pops could tell if I was lying or telling the truth though. I used to try and avoid eye contact with him, so he couldn't read my eyes. In all realness, both of my parents knew when I was bulls**ting!!!

*****

April of 1987, I finally caught up to the trouble that was laying ahead of me in my chase for this composite sketch of manhood that I had mindlessly envisioned myself developing into. Over the period of time that I spent building up this ego-fueling reputation, I had created a few enemies. I mean, these were some dudes that really wanted my head. Because of my destroyed relationship with J-Doe, I fought numerous of times on Washington St., Adams St., Carmen's, or just while I was walking down Delaware Ave. Win, lose or draw, we were "getting right" (fighting) though. My biological father, 'Louie', was tough, loved boxing and encouraged his kids to protect themselves at all costs. My step-pop, 'Robert' was a tough brother too! He was more of a man who used mental before physical though.

One evening Mando, this dude named 'I.V.' and myself were returning to the town from Philly. We stopped at my house for a brief moment, so I could make a few phone calls. One of those calls was Spank, confirming the arrival of 2 cars that I had parked in the Mannor Apts. Remembering that there was a basketball game at the high school, we agreed to walk to it and see what was good. As we walked on Delaware St., a few feet from Carmen's, people were coming our way from that direction. I wanted to go into Carmen's to get something to eat. Out of all the individuals I could run into, it was Mighty. 'Mighty', 'Polo', 'Bill', 'Blast' and 'E.M.'. They were all seniors in high school except for Mighty. He was expelled from school for sniffing "raw" (cocaine) in class, and again in the gymnasium. I disliked this dude.

Two years before this day, Mighty and I went at each other hard, fighting on my block. Swedesboro Ave. was a 24 hour a day, 7 day a week drug block, and he ran coke for an old-head out there named 'Trickey'. Even though I was slick with my mouth, sarcastic and cruel when my buttons were pushed, I was humble. However, Mighty decided to hurl insults my way. When I threw something slicker back at him, all of his "so-called" boy laughed, which angered and crushed his ego, especially being that he was older than me. So he punched me in my face, but I didn't drop. I grabbed a brick, and tried to kill him with it...

So now, back at Carmen's tensions were brewing! I knew in my heart that something was going to go down. Words and curses were violently exchanged back and forth. With my cousin and I.V. with me, I was thinking I was good. I.V. ended up getting tossed up in the air and body-slammed hard! Then Mando ran as the rest of the group circled me. Alone and outnumbered, I made an executive decision to follow Mando's lead, and I jetted. When I got about a block away, I made an almost fatal mistake. I circled a car, because Polo (who was fast as a Cheetah) caught up to me. The rest were gaining on me as I booked towards a fence. Mighty was the first to sneak me. I called him a pu**y as he landed another blow. I just started swinging relentlessly! Getting jumped by dudes (if they know what they're doing) is no joke, but these dudes were soft!

When I got home, Mom Dukes started going off as soon as I walked over the threshold. "What happened to you?!?" You know how mothers are, all overprotective and trained to go for their children. I told her I got jumped, and this infuriated her! The way she responded, I thought that she was going to grab my pops gun and say, "Come on! Not my son! We're going to look for them..." (LOL!) Not my mom's though. She said, "Hell no! Not my son! We're going to the police station!"

I didn't want to be known for having anything to do with the police and end up getting labeled a snitch. That wasn't a good look for anyone in the streets. As far as I was concerned, I was building up my street credibility. So I had something more sinful and vicious in mind. This was the very first time that I had a predominate thought to carry out an act of murder!

The next morning arrived with lack of sleep being a burden. My mind was a retrograding mess! I was only missing one thing, the gun! The evils that had infiltrated my logical sense of being were now driving me. I took my pops .357 handgun on many occasions. Dating back to Summerset Hills, I grew an infatuation for guns.

Fat-Joe, Lee, 'Rakim' and I all walked to school together as we always did. I'll tell y'all about Rakim later. Anyway though, we piled in Carmen's so I could buy my favorite candies (Swedish Fish and Sour Patch Kids), and play a quick game of pinball as usual. My eye was a bit tinted from being jumped so many questions were asked by my peers. This only infuriated me even more! I stopped playing the game and called my boys to the corner to show them the gun. These were all my boys (or so I thought) so this wasn't the first time they saw it or heard me speak of wanting to use it. Having a strap on school grounds was a totally ingenuous act that was unheard of in my day. Fat-Joe attempted to warn me against shooting these dudes, but the devil had already assisted me in making up my mind though. I was definitive in my quest to transfer my pain over to whoever! First period, with the gun in my bookbag, I walked to the seniors lockers and hallway. In my purview Polo and E.M. were lurking. A brief back and forth argument ensued. I reached into my bookbag and gripped the gun just as a teacher came into the hallway, interrupting what was going on and probably saving a life or two. I was told to get where I belong.

In Ms. Cee and Vee's class second period, Mr. Mont, Mr. Demone and a security presence barged in, escorting me out and to the principal's office. I wondered what this could be for? It was a long walk to the principal's office! When we got in the office, the principal claimed that I had a firearm on school grounds, which I persisted to deny. There wasn't any way out of this though. I was busted! The principal zipped open my backpack and pulled out the snub nose .357.

"Jesus! What the hell are you doing with this?" the principal roared.

I just shrugged my shoulders as if to say, "I don't know..." For this noxious act of idiocy, I was given 5 years of probation, 50 hours of community service and a $100 fine. Oh yeah, and of course I was expelled from the high school.

*****

In certain moments in time, I get and have gotten stuck in my own narrow patterns of consistent in competencies curved into reckless abandonment and selfishness. A lack of community worth was also a diagnosis that I suffered from. I was headed down a slippery slope of trouble, undermining the very foundation of my youth, purpose and potential! I never saw my own strengths or my weaknesses in a balanced light. Everything negative in my psyche exaggerated things, becoming its own idolatry; stealing space of occupancy. I was burdened for years to come, not knowing who I was becoming or what I had already become. So much of what I heard and saw, also what I hadn't heard and saw, for the entire truth of my novice life thus far was a mold for my road to greater failures and even successes. They say that we live, and we learn, and indeed we do! I just had to learn everything the hard way. Hard-headed is not a strong enough word for what I was!

*****

"A moral virtue is a habit that enables a human being to live according to reason!"

-Aristotle

"What is reason?" should've been the initial question asked by my inquisitive mind! Nevertheless, had I been adherent to the biological factor of what is called "Cognitive Auditory" that is developed at 15 years young. The processing of the above of weaknesses. In fact, in contrast, my understanding of the fictional world I was intrigued by would never have become such an invidious and inveterate circumstance. I would not have physically become an awarded species to be a *hypothecation* in New Jersey's busy institutional/financial (prison) wall of schemes!

By happenstance, the lack thereof led me to more immense and greater ignorance, stupidity and crimes. In the thick of all this, I was also selfishly bringing hurt and pain to others, mostly the people who loved me the most. (smh!)

Perhaps if I armed myself with the acuity provided via the sights and sounds of the more positive and actuated I would have never been subjugated to criminality the many moral, ethical, spiritual and racial covenants that my lineage has counted me in on since Genesis!

Unfortunately, barriers began to amount between my family and I. However, my relationships with the streets, crime and women were apparent. I had not reserved any common sense as to view the depth of a mark of a criminal record that I was beginning to incur. The Cost of leaning on my own understanding did not register at this time.

My *egregious* actions were *fastuous* and discordant, which forced those around me to address the issues that sustained or evoked some type of feelings. Granted, some would still end up setting aside time to support me in striving to understand. "Why?"

*****

After the dealings with the criminal punishment and slave system while on probation status, I was still in route of self-discovery. I was also still in continuance of self-greed, being an embarrassment to my family and lying to them in an attempt to keep my dealings in the streets a secret. I don't know who I thought I was fooling though.

With being expelled from school, I had too much time on my hands to raise hell in the community. Stealing cars and selling drugs had become somewhat of a profession of mine. Like, I really

66

thought I could make a living and do this stuff forever. I was blinded by the illusory of the fame that I saw and admired in the stages of searching and trying to find my way in life.

There were these groggy types of days that I would demand some alone time and just sit around thinking of my humanitarian value. I would ask myself, "What am I on this earth for?" I would curse life and the people who made life the way that it was for myself and my loved ones!

I didn't have it in me to open up with my moms and pops. I saw them as going through their own struggles, trying to beat the weight of a caste system that black folks were emotionally, psychologically, racially and economically in. As my parents went about their implementation of their contributions to an industrial work force, I unintentionally refrained from asking too many questions. I would later regret not asking some of those questions that I had in mind, because I know now that my parents would have given me their critical thoughts and intelligent answers which could have set me on a more constructive path. But I was drowning in my own sorrow!

One can be raised in a good household with parents that are providing and striving to do the best they can. Although they raise us the best way they know how, marks of reality are still missed because of the many inequalities that we face daily, created by the Jim Crow System that keeps us working extra hard try and become equal. We have not really been emancipated. The Black race has been casualties and victims of oppression since the Atlantic Slave Trade. What was written in Proclamation of Emancipation and parts of the United States Constitution that were supposed to be in our favor have been distorted and eradicated to keep us down and fighting an uphill battle against the oppressor. The sad part about this is that if we don't al wake up we will never win! We must come together, teach each other (each one, teach one), realize that we are at war, and arm ourselves with knowledge as our swords. We will climb the hill that way and make our way to the finer things as a strong unit!

I was one of the blind, more so on the destructive side of things. I was a walking example of division, unconsciously assisting in the system's conquering! As counterproductive as my actions were, you couldn't tell me that back then. As a Black youth, I was appointed traditional character traits to respectfully protect the family and the community from these said, "unnatural behaviors" and "unnatural cultures" that have plagued our demographic for centuries. This couldn't be, because I couldn't even protect myself from such things. I was such these "such things" that I speak of. Amerikkka colors its agendas in law and policy. Then criminality is forged to get us to go against these laws and policies, so they can punish us with a lifetime in their modern-day slave camps, prison!

People in the neighborhood knew that I was willing to handle a gun and there was a chance that they could get shot. Because of this, it made it easier for me to sell a sinuous lifestyle that kept people off balance. Then again, some were not fooled, and others didn't even care.

CHAPTER V

"PRIMARY ISSUES!"

September of 1987, I was ripping up and down the streets and highways on a Yamaha FJ 1100 street bike. This was my first time riding on a bike with such power. Back then, if you had a bike, especially one of this stature you were getting all the girls. I would always around and attract a numerous amount of both girls my age and even grown women.

One day, I decided to ride down to West Philly on a solo mission. That day I bought a few things from The Gallery. I knew I shouldn't have been in this area, but my thirst for west Philly's women needed to be quenched. The area of 52nd and Market was jumping, so I made 52nd and Market my focal point.

At the light, 2 females pulled up. I followed them to 58th and Baltimore, because of their beauty. I felt safe from harm with a .38 snub nose on me that Spank's boy sold me. Allow me to infuse the facts of this organized confusion: I'm riding around on a stolen motor cycle, a stolen and unregistered gun on me with no permit to carry, a pocket full of money, and I was meeting up with women that I didn't know in a neighborhood that should have been out of my comfort zone. But my tough behind didn't care! All I saw was fun, fun and more fun. I was going to get money, have sex with as many females as I was attracted to and have as much fun as I could possibly have, no matter what THE COST! My trip over to these girl's house almost cost me my life!

Back in the 80's, dark skinned dudes were vastly jealous of lighter skinned brothers! Unfortunately, one of their friends, a dark-skinned brother, (I'm guessing he was from their area) started talking slick and coming at me sideways while we were in these girl's house. So I talked even slicker. He tried to swing on me, and we started scuffling and wrestling. After slamming him, I was able to whip out my gun. He saw the gun, he froze then ran outside. The females followed behind him and started cursing the boy out. He was one of those big, Black ugly type dudes too! He probably fights himself when he looks in the mirror. My mind continued to manifest shooting this brother. The females tried to apologize to me, but in my eyes, they were attempting to set me up to get robbed and possibly my behind kicked or killed. West Philly girls were good for that. The voice inside of my head was telling me to shoot these chicks for trying to set me up.

As I got back on my bike and pulled off shots were fired coming from behind me. I looked back and the dude that I had just whipped out on was with his boys, shooting at me. It was more than one gun too as you could tell from the succession of rapid fire that was erupting.

I made it out of that situation with my life, but what if I would've stayed over their house a few seconds later? The snub nose .38 that I had on me only had 6 shots. I was outnumbered and outgunned. If a shoot-out between us would have ensued, what would have been my chances for survival?

Reaching deeper, innocent bystanders could have been hit in the midst of this senseless madness. It could've been somebody's child, someone's grandmother or sister...

After this close encounter, I returned home after parking the motor cycle at my boy Chance's mom's house. She got high on cocaine. So I was able to hit her with a bag or 2 here and there.

Approximately 2 days later, I was arrested for the stolen bike. Normally, I would outrun the police on it. I mean, the bike tapped speeds of 160 miles per hour, and on many occasions, I maxed its potential. Unfortunately, on this day, I let someone else operate the bike.

When he noticed the police, he pulled over. I was a manipulative and persuasive young dude. So I knew how to persuade someone my lack of involvement in whatever trouble I was facing. I told the police that a fiend sold it to me for 25 bags of cocaine and that I wasn't aware of it being stolen. By law, you can't actually be charged with grand theft auto or receiving stolen property, but I was charged with theft by conveyance. So knowing that bit of the law got us charged with the lesser crime. I am not promoting this idiotic, manipulative behavior either. I'm just pointing out the reasoning that I used.

My parents having to take trips to the police station to pick me up had become like a norm. Yeah, I was embarrassing and disappointing my parents. Not really knowing the full extent and harm of my actions, this was just another reaction to my malign standards of living.

I continued unlimitedly in my criminal expedition, from selling drug and stealing cars, to even robbing. My forged relationship with Spank started to crumble, and I began to see the illusions that this game had. I started realizing that the streets and people around me that claimed to be something synonymous to family were really only dealing with me for their own personal gain. It called to mind everything that my pops expressed to me about "friends"...

One thing about the streets is that they teach you how to read people in many ways. I became very attentive when dealing with people to sense their intentions, but I must admit that I didn't catch everything.

The world-renowned author Robert Greene said, "Never put too much trust in friends, learn how to use enemies. Be wary of friends-they will betray you more quickly, for they are easily aroused to envy... hire a former enemy and he will be more loyal, because he has more to prove..."

I began to shed a lot of the novice stripes and acquire some common sense. All the cars I had stolen for Spank and his associates still seemed to leave me vexed and contemplating a "joux" (robbery). Feelings of apprehension and curiosity shook my mind. I was feeling this way because Spank's words began to consist of just words with no action behind them. His eyes weren't matching his smile at all. Money was owed to me, and my patience was growing extremely thin. This may sound stereotypical, but I was really thinking about doing something to harm dude!

Considering the dirt that Spank and I had already done together, I knew he wasn't going to like my new decision. He assisted me in taking care of some things that we vowed to never discuss. However, in all reality, I was just being used.

I started to over-generalize and have stereotypical thinking. I was seeing everyone the same and dividing the world into groups and categories. To me, everyone had the same values, characteristics, qualities and aims. No one was an individual with their own special personality in my screwed up mind. This way of thinking happened to be a result of the company I kept. The people you surround yourself with rub off on you!

I told Spank that I wasn't feeling what we had going on anymore. What was going on wasn't what I thought it was in the beginning, nor was it what we initially discussed. He adamantly tried to assure me that some changes would be made to better the situation. I didn't want to hear none of that though! I was done. He also owed me money, and I wanted mine!

Despite our cutting ties, Spank continued to act like we were cool, however, that wasn't so. If he truly had an invested common interest, then he would have honored as a contractual entity.

Several days later, back at Fat-Joe's house, one of Fat-Joe's family acquaintances visited, and I paid his presence no mind at all. I saw the boy around before, but I never peaced him. From the stories FatJoe told me about dude, I was highly suspicious of him. Fat-Joe and Lee were now partnered up and knee-deep in the drug game with teams of runners and even had this old head under the wing that cooked up their coke. These were my dudes, and I should have been linked in with them before anybody, but my priorities were nonexistent. I honestly didn't know what I wanted to do with myself. I was lost! I didn't know if I wanted to be a drug dealer, a stick-up kid, car-thief, or a plain old gangster! In retrospect, I was literally destroying myself in my attempts to acquire a name. What the hell was I looking for a name for? My mother already gave me a name!!!

In the meantime and between time, the state had ordered me to go to this alternative school in Atco, NJ. The place was a just as bad, actually it was even worse than Somerset Hills! It was full of the baddest teenagers from different areas and hoods. This school was supposed to be to change us, but no one there had any intention on changing their ways! It was a population of young gangsters.

I now had to manage my time with this school mess (that I felt as though was in the way) and the streets. I started spending more time over Fat-Joe's house. I wanted in on what him and Lee had going on! You know how that goes... You really start to measure yourself up to the people around you. Then, in an internal attempt of convictional condemnation, you feel out of place when you're not measuring up. Lee had once said to me, "Yo, you into too much s**t! One minute you f**kin' wit' us, then the next minute you wit' the ni@@a in Philly..."

I eventually ended up speaking with Doe and clearing things up. I could have been wrong, but I felt like he was more relaxed with me considering the talk around the hood with all of my associations with different criminal excursions. Plus, the streets were still talking about me bringing that gun to school. I even spoke to Doe about doing something to the dude Spank. Being that Doe was from the Germantown section of Philly, he had a few connects. Our discussion on Spank didn't really go anywhere though. I needed to form an alliance with goons that were just as raw or greater than Spank anyway though.

Soon thereafter, Fat-Joe started getting calls from Spank, like FatJoe was still on board with him. Fat-Joe reiterated to Spank that he was done with him. So both Fat-Joe and I put Spank behind us and concentrated our focus more so on what lie before us.

I was centralized on the fact that my new endeavor would materialize in prime fashion. In all actuality, I should have been centered in truth!

73

Fat-Joe and I had rode up to the West Oak Lane section of Philly to visit a female friend that I met at the City Blues clothing store. We had rented a Chrysler Lebaron, giving a fiend 4 bags to put his John Hancock on the rental papers for us. I went to my female friend's crib and did some smoking and drinking. Then, we had sex, and I vacated.

I ended up calling Spank. I didn't call because I wanted to chill with dude or anything like that, but because he still owed me money, and of course I still wanted mine!

In my mind and heart, titles never really meant anything to me. My view of all people was basically the same. I was very cynical. Therefore, everyone was approachable in my eyes and bled the same way that I bled. Spank was no exception! To be totally truthful, I had no win! I was over my head, because he had more goons under him than I did of course. However, I learned that if you're perceived as soft in the streets, or any street setting for that matter, then people will run over you. And my pride and ego would not allow anyone to just run over me. That was out!!!

Somehow Fat-Joe and I wound up heading over to West Philly. Fat-Joe attempted to push me away from my thoughts, telling me that I didn't need that money, but he obviously didn't see things the way I seen them. We pulled up to the store on the corner of 54th & Landsdown, where Spank, this dude named True and 2 other dudes were. Fat-Joe tries again to change my mind about approaching this situation but to no avail. I was fixed on acquiring my respect by any means necessary!

I jumped out and went to talk to Spank about this money he owed me, and our conversation wasn't going well at all. Both of us were growing frustrated with each other. When a man (or young man) starts to rapidly talk with his hands, voices get raised and noses start flaring, physical action usually follows. The boy true tried to swing on me, but I dipped it. True didn't like me anyway. A little while ago, I put him in a sleeper hold from a bet that was made. Dude had no fight game though. Spank tried to swing on Fat-Joe. The other 2 dudes on the block tried to attack. I heard 2 shots fired, and I froze for a split second, looking around to see if I or Fat-Joe was shot. Then I heard, "Click-click-click..." This negro tried to shoot us, and the gun jammed. On top of that, he missed which ever one of us he was trying to hit when he let off those 2 shots.

"This pu**y tried to kill us!" I exclaimed. I then pulled out the .38 that I had in my back pocket....

We were able to get in the car and head back over to West Oak Lane, but Fat-Joe wanted to get back to Jersey. The funny thing about this is that, Fat-Joe continuously told me not to shoot them, but I wanted to light all of their candles (shoot them in the head). I was not my natural self anymore! No longer was I who I was raised to be. I was now playing the role of this facade that I had created! My anger and blame only contributed to the cycle of wrong that I had already partook in. More bad energy was generated, and no real solutions were brought about.

I would try to deny the shadows of anger to my mother, but it only made my anger stronger and darker. However, I created a core story that either casted me in the role of the victim or the role of the perpetrator. Under the weight of disappointment and learned helplessness, my family continued to experience the downside of my criminal nonsense.

I never realized that I held the power to unlearn my anger and other destructive ways. I could have exchanged the victim and the perp in for truth and authenticity. Who I was, was not who I had the potential to be.

*****

In the next few months to come, unfortunately just about every criminal charge was bestowed upon me, embarrassing my family yet again. April of 1988, the fate of a fox met his trap on his trails. Finally, my reign had come to an end! I now consider it being rescued instead of arrested. I was caught by Paulsboro Police sleeping in a stolen BMW, drunk and high off an immoderate amount of marijuana.

In a strange sense of relief, this arrest was contingent upon my conscience, considering all that I had put my family through. Loved ones like my grandparents, parents and even my sister covered me in prayers while worrying about my wellbeing, and all I gave them was more reasons to worry. I would do things like leave home for days and sometimes weeks on end, and my family wouldn't know if I was dead or alive, in jail or hospitalized!

Contrary to popular traditional values of communication, my ignorance and self-righteous indignation prevented me from embracing my complicity in the hurt my family endured. Thinking back gives me a disturbing observation of this truth!

In the wake of my actions, all went wrong due to my intrinsic behaviors, my mother would come to visit me in Clarksboro Juvenile Detention Center, in Mt. Royal, NJ. Yeah, her son was in another security institution.

Fact: Jails and prisons, whether juvenile or adult, differ in the types of inmates they house, the locations and their size and what types of programs they have or lack thereof. Jails are locally administered facilitated slave camps that secure bodies (bonds) for corporate capital. Prisons nevertheless are administered by either state or federal government authority all backed by many corporate-political interests. Typically, these prisons hold men and (or) women sentenced to terms of confinement for more than a year.

Note: Prisons tend to be located away from dense areas and claim to have rehabilitation programs fit for men and women's needs.

In penning these facts, present was a resurgence of an in-depth conversation with my mother at visit. We spoke freely of the state and conditions that us Black folks were in-how a well-qualified Black person can equally possess an impressive resume as his or her white counterpart or better and the job will automatically be given to the white person.

At 16 years old, I was becoming cognizant of the issues in light of my ignorance to my behavior, actions and whom I persisted to disappoint in the midst of all my nonsense. The white man this... The white man that... Blah! Blah! Blah! My mother would respond to my adolescent inquiries as efficient as she was able to. Prior to, my pops would always manifest, "Don't expect me to visit a jail, because I work in one..." And none of this wisdom was diacritical from any other moments I heard this. I became a victim of my own self. I'd go on to be released and back in the detention center a month later for drug charges and another stolen car. I was released again and returned in another month, but this time the system would become my fate, trapped in securities where friendships are manipulated, conversations and concerns are meaningless, love is feigned, and humanity is undermined by staff/police.

*****

In August of 1988, I was placed in a court ordered residential program called Southern Prep, in Little Egg Harbor, NJ. Four weeks in, I left the program for the idiotic reasons of chasing a female! I'd met this young lady when I was in Clarksboro. She was incarcerated as well. The staff trusted me to the point where they would allow me to go over to the girls side of the jail to play cards with them and talk. I had what they called and still to this day call "juice", which is when you're highly favored and able to maneuver in ways that others weren't. This young lady and I, who I will call C.T., would engage in sexual acts with the other girls as our look-outs. Since Deasia and the other females that I hadn't couldn't come visit me or give me what I needed, the same behavior I perpetuated on the streets continued in the facilities.

I was caught a mile away from the Southern Prep and returned back to the program until the sheriffs picked me up, taking me back to Clarksboro Detention Center.

Now, I was by far reduced to a force of paralysis and unable to maneuver, function, or motivate my humanity leveled with a consistent want and desire. Being unable to do as I wanted by way

77

of dictatorial factors, I was feeling sickly, and I began to reject the notion of change...

I would do things like purposely not lock in my cell, which forced the staff to call the sheriffs who were next door. They would come to know me by name as this was a regular event of mine. We would fight, wrestle, and when they got the best of me (as they always did), they would drag me to my cell.

I worked out religiously. So I was not an average size 16 year old. At 16 I had knocked out numerous of grown men, and I was still chasing the recognition. "Who was I?" and "Who was I to others?"

September 1988, I was about to spend a sum of my life in the first juvenile state ran slave camp. No more sexual excursions, driving, shopping, family cookouts, a comfortable bed, the constant voice of my mother, father, sister and other family. I was now subject to an entire different authority! I was officially a number! This was The Cost of my ignorance. D. Preme Norman was now known as Slave# 38782!

I would be remised if in fact I failed to share again the effects that my decisions and confinement had on my loved ones. I loved my family, and this revelation was proclaimed by a deceptive inner perception. Well, I claimed to have loved them, but my actions said otherwise. I lacked self-love! No matter how much I missed my family and professed it, I was very much incapable of initiating the reciprocal dynamics required to consummate any expression of truth.

My education was dire in its languishing. I was still trying to seek who and what to be. The atmosphere of this new facility, Skillman Corrections for Juveniles, in Skillman, New Jersey, happened to be an objectionable fate of change for me! Drugs, fights, and they even housed girls there. Teachers barely taught, because they were really scared of us. Teachers would get beat up and disrespected to the point where class was just a meeting place. On the units, we fought on what is called blacktop. The corrections officers loved to watch us literally participate in war games against each other.

As for myself, I was huge for my age. You would think that would've kept the wolves away, however, the dudes that wanted "rec" (action) that made me a target. I was the one that you could make a name off of if you could manage to beat me up, because of my size, but I was far from an easy win!

When my time started nearing its end, I still hadn't consciously addressed not one of the errors that led me to this trial of a road in my life...

The dungeons that they call cells, in which myself and others spent time in. Sadly, the recognition of a strong and dangerous fruit that I bared (the corrupted apple), led to one conclusion, and that was my definition of an emotionless feeling! I would always feel this state of loneliness, and I also felt misunderstood. I needed some sort of refuge! But where could I seek refuge? I didn't have readily internal instruments to seek the necessary change that would assist in addressing my ethical, social and historical abandonment.

Not able to stay out of trouble, I went to The New Jersey Training School for Boys, better known as Jamesburg. I was placed in their lock-up for 15 days on 23 hours a day lock down in one of their 6x9 dungeons. Coming out of lock-up, I kept at the facility and housed on cottage 7, which at the time was a sports dorm, directly in front of the football field. The coach for football team, Coach Holmes, observed me days later throwing the football around, and he admired my arm. After inquiring about how much time I had left (which was a year due to all of the trouble I had gotten into), he presented an offer for me to play for him. With nothing else to do and being a natural athlete, I decided to play. Not only was Coach Holmes a good coach, but a good mentor as well.

It wasn't hard at all to find a fight on cottage 7, given the poor management of my anger. In my mind and heart, I was the closest thing to unbeatable! However, one week into my stay on cottage 7, I met my match. It was a brother from Patterson, NJ. He was said to be the toughest dude on the cottage, and he picked up the vibe of my dislike for him immediately. He was a bully, and I hated bullies with a passion! I felt like, when you hate someone the best thing to do was to provoke them to fight, which is exactly what I did. In front of everyone, we fought like barbarian warriors. Even the corrections officers stood in attendance as we got busy. This ended up being a brave loss for me, but I vowed never to lose again! From that day on, cottage 7 knew who I was...

*****

In The Souls of Black Folk W.E.B DuBois said: "To the real question, how does it feel to be a problem? I answer seldom a word. And yet, being a problem is a strange experience-peculiar even for one who has never been anything else, say perhaps in boyhood and Europe."

*****

Myself and 2 other guys escaped from Jamesburg. For the entire 2 weeks on the loose from the devil's lasso, I involved myself in countless criminal exertions in between Newark, Camden and Philly. I had rekindled the flame that I had with Cinda prior to my incarceration. She assisted in convincing me to turn myself in to complete my sentence. Of course, there were many declines regarding her concerns.

My physical composition had literally begun to wear down due to the way I had been abusing my body. On the run, I was living that nocturnal life, partying, drinking, smoking weed, having sex, selling drugs, doing stick-ups and stealing cars.

Precisely a day after Cinda's plea for me to turn myself in, I was apprehended. I was returned back to the state's custody, where I was given 15 days in lock-up along with a Superior Court indictment for an escape charge. They threw an extra year on my sentence.

I was shipped to another one of the Department of Correction's slave camps in Bordentown, NJ called, J.M.S.F (Juvenile Medium Security Facility). This spot was also known as "Baby Bordentown", or "Gladiator School". The real Bordentown was a young adult correctional facility where it went down at. They called J.M.S.F Baby Bordentown, because it went down, and they called it Gladiator

School, because if you didn't come in a Gladiator, you would surely leave one! This spot would end up contributing to further suppressing the emotional issues that hid deep within me.

New Jersey's (just like the rest of this corporate country's securities) approach to punishment reveals its soul and means, how "it" (government) understands cause and responsibility; what its utopian hopes are; and how it has decided to approach many conflicts that have been created by way of the way they marginalize us (Blacks and Hispanics) into such densely populated urban areas. Four questions need be truthfully addressed, why, in the sense of "What Cost?"; Why, in a sense of "What purpose?"; How and What? Perhaps, these questions should open up Athenian punishment in many ways that convey a living society that continually made choices about how to construct authority. The story about Athens should by way of contrast provoke your own thoughts about how punishment serves the construction of not just the authority, but more importantly, the modern minority. However, just like the Athens, this country including New Jersey's legislative, executive and judicial body's institution of modern democracies allows the anger of its citizens and (or) their interests in them to convert their moment of private anger into public decisions, crafted with a view of curing the community and the "special financial interests" through a restoration of peace and at The Cost of taxpayer's money. However, as well... an accurate description of social, economic and racial policies, when in the "ode to man" of Blackness in Amerikkka and courts having been praised by "them". For we have assimilated to their culture, not genetically or historically, but psychologically. Sadly... we punished our own Black selves/people from the disease of anger and distrust holding trial on prosecution/persecution of our own, as the Athens country does. If we were to ask any modern citizen to explain why modern states use imprisonment as their preferred penalty he or she will reply, "We need to keep the bad people off the streets! Prisons are for deterrents!" Or maybe the odds will turn out just as good that a recognized answer will be, "Prisons are places where a man or woman individually receives the proper ineffective mental, emotional, and educational help needed, get religion (if choose to) and hold a job, learn a skillset, learn leadership skills, learn family functioning and so be referred for their reentry to their community to never return!"

In 1989, the Bureau of Justice statistics predicted that incarceration rates would dramatically rise from 5.1% that is likely to do time to 9.0% to be incarcerated at least once during a life span, and Black men 28.5% are 6 times as likely as white men (4.4%) to be imprisoned as followed by Hispanic men, which is 16% likely. For decades, Blacks and Hispanics have disproportionally represented the countries prison system. Alarmingly we represent more than half of the prison system.

Of this population, unfortunately many enter the system very much uneducated with less than an 8th education, low quality communication skills and the stigma of emotional, social, as well as economic issues. Now, populate a slave camp with these facts as dense as can be and you will have witnessed the "rats in the box theory" (how the cities projects/apartment dwelling are constructed. To say the least... BJS (The Bureau of Justice Statistics) along with legislative, executive and judicial bodies in total disregard failed to statistically bethink of the "why's" followed with individual "solutions" to the failure of young Black and Hispanic individuals from an empathetic psyche.

J.M.S.F was really just another oppressive warehouse for young boys. A place that encouraged boys to rep their towns, work out, trash talk to one another, and when that got old we would fight or sometimes there would be a combination of 2 towns rioting against one another. The atrocious scenes of stabbings and young Black and Hispanic heads being busted literally to the white meat, eyeballs knocked out, and the massive leakage of blood, etc...

There were single rooms, so I would have some breaks from the craziness to reflect on family and friends that I missed. In my absence, I thought to myself, very few people answered the call of true friendship. I was thinking what kind of friends I had, and did I correctly make a proper assessment that they even were in fact, real friends! I was lost, admittedly in need to be accepted or to feel as though I was somebody. During my street days, I would get high, sell drugs, associate with numerous women and steal cars. I even thought at times I was the life of the party when in all actuality the party would have life with or without me! If you would've let me tell it though, I was the party! I was not capable of identifying true friendship or who I really was. I was too sick in my thoughts to see life for what it really was. For I seen it as I was!

Still selling myself short, I continued to choose the exact same friends, absent in conjunction with a total lack of communication while I was in J.M.S.F. I would lie to my mother saying that I was meaningfully putting my time to use and that I was working towards a brighter future for myself, one of significance and value. I wasn't really working on nothing!

Despite the results of my past behaviors and lengthy period of lies, I still received visits from my mother, grandmother, grandfather and sister. Family versus pseudo-friendships should have been a no brainer, especially considering all of the drama I had been through with individuals in these meaningless "friendships". Family offers so much more solace than one could imagine. Still I didn't change.

Amazingly, I was released but with one year of strict juvenile parole conditions. Would you like an authentic definition of what I was released to??? In my departure from J.M.S.F I hadn't learned a productive thing! Just like all of the other facilities that I had been housed in, the lack of communication between the facilitators and the teachers, lack of common concern and insight, the lack of importance in the family and community and fear to be different! At the end, I was really the loser! Recidivism is real!

CHAPTER VI

"PSYCHOLOGICAL CONJUNCTURE: WHY PEACE WAS HARD TO COME BY..."

My grandmother would always accept me with open arms, no matter what I had done wrong. As a child, I loved how she would smother me with so much love from the second she saw me and how her actions never withered. My family's words of wisdom that were delivered to me through visitations and jail phone calls still rang rapidly throughout my head. Nevertheless, I was egregiously involved in the common negatives that plagued the Black communities. I was right back involved with my unproductive "pseudo-friends", the same ones that didn't even reach out to me when I was down and out. I was induced by the peer pressure, blinded to the reality of my freedom being at stake as long as this voice of division continued in its attack.   The irony of this all was that, I saw all fake things as true and all true things as fake... Friends versus Family...

My mother was trusting and kind enough to secure a job for me with her at Harcourt Blace & Jovaneuich, a very large book distribution company. I was given a position in the warehouse, I had psychologically adapted to waking up at the crack of dawn during my stint in the slave camps, because in their meals have no waiting list. Furthermore, my pops instilled that in me early in my childhood. Sleeping in wasn't an easy feat considering the fact that my sister and I would have to do chores. Yeah, my parent played no games when it came to keeping the house together! I had become very handy around the house thanks to my moms and pops. I was also very handy at work. However, I failed to refrain from the streets, the women and the drug dealing...

I was dealing with a female named 'Roslyn', from the Logan section of Philly. My cousin 'Lisset' had introduced us during my time in J.M.S.F. Roslyn had a wonderful, humble and gorgeous make-up. I would go on to love her and strive to step my manhood up for her. In hindsight, I should have began with mastering boyhood before taking that leap. How was I to be the man that she needed me to be?

In 1990, there was a sudden surge in the drug game. While I was gone, Lee had risen to a mysterious peak in success. Fat Joe had moved back to Philly and started politicking with 2 brothers from Abersford Projects. Mando connected with a dude named 'Kay', who had a Euro Sport with an orchestra in it. Jazzo had the BMW 745 and the Cadillac. Jose was styling in the new Maxima, and Lee had the Audi. Everyone had stepped their game up, and you know I wanted in by all means. They were shining hard, but I would later come to realize that, "everything that glitters isn't gold!"

Seeing dudes in herringbone chains, Alpina glasses, the new 3 quarter Gucci's and new cars... Man, I wanted what I wanted, and I was going to get it! Roslyn was even more motivation for me to chase this shine, because when your girlfriend shines, everyone sees it, and you get the credit and recognition for it.

*****

Waist Deep was the description of my involvement. I started digging into the goldmines of the drug trade. "The opportunity of defeating the enemy is provided by the enemy himself", said the great Chinese war general Sun Tzu.

At least I can say that while I was in juvenile prison I became privy to tactical books that helped advance my criminal mind and objectives for the future. I read Sun Tzu's The Art Of War, Robert Greene's 48 Laws Of Power and other books on manipulating situations. I infected my mind with strategic values, plans, goals and endeavors predicated on my numbers game plan, whether financially or on a level of humanity.

J-Doe was still grinding between Germantown and Paulsboro. While I was gone a lot had changed as far as the way drug dealers were managing things. Everyone was independent for the most part. Doe was not supplying the demand anymore. Dudes were copping their weight from North Philly now. This in fact made it easier and more profitable for me as well! My female friend from West Oak Lane, we had become an item. Her brother 'Sparty Rock', from Logan, was in the loop heavy with prominent people in parts of the city. I planned on forging a relationship with Sparty-Rock so I could get in where I fit in!

I was advanced in my thinking, wanting to step up to a higher level in the game. I transferred my dreams into a reality while I was in J.M.S.F. The number of young men that surrounded my thinking in continuous fashions constantly pitched street stories back and forth. We called these stories "Beatdowns". When someone was telling you a story, they were beating you down. Dudes beat down just about all day. Young men from all walks of life and parts of Jersey, like Camden, Newark, Patterson, Jersey City and the small towns like Paulsboro, Woodbury, and Asbury Park. There were even some dudes from out of state like Philly, New York and North Carolina. With the versatile diction of life that people brought, what was unknown about certain things was made known through these other walks of life. No matter the attempts of positive family influence and love, the ego, the pride and the psychological issues that I was dealing with trumped the historical truth and the hegemony thereof.

A crib on Fairhill and Cambria was one of my Bro's spots. It was a regular house where women would cook for you, you could play Sega, listen to mixtapes and wait for your coke. It tok 30 to 45 minutes for them to run across town to acquire the product and come back.

Prison also taught me how to better negotiate and maneuver, and make connections with the people around me. Being well at attaining knowledge was helpful in my efforts to rise beyond who I was to make more money. I had to grow into the person that I wanted to be.

Shockingly, the rapidity of my rise in the drug game exceeded my expectations. I literally went from a quarter ounce of coke that Lee gave me on consignment to a quarter "bird" (kilo) in no time! I had the presence of mind to notice that drug dealers from small South Jersey towns would pay $30 a gram for weight of cocaine. I was paying $20 a gram, which was 3 points off the regular price, considering the amount that I was purchasing and finding a way to manipulate the game to make it work better for me. I negotiated with my homie that ran this house on Fairhill and Cambria. They began to give me coke on consignment to sell. I didn't have to spend my own money to make a flip. So it was a win win for me!

I wanted to live comfortably being that I was in an state ran institutions over the years. I could never get on right and stay right, but because I had become fortuitous enough to acquire a semiconscious of what it meant to be Black here in Amerikkka. The acquisition of money, females, cars, clothes and friends was within my limited understanding of living comfortably.

Still living under the roof of my parents, I maintained my lies, deceit and manipulativeness. I was living a completely separate and different life from what they thought I was living.

My friend, who I will now introduce as 'Portia'. from West Oak Lane now lived in Camden, NJ, and I was capable of financially holding my own. All of the things that my moms and pops couldn't afford to buy me in the past, I could now buy for myself, and the places that i couldn't travel to or go, I now could!

I had an optical sense of the world being one big empty canvas that I was painting from the soul of Michael Angelo...

*****

One night in June while sitting in the car with Lee at Camden High park, where everybody would go to hang-out, bump their systems and mingle with females. I was a little drunk high on marijuana. Lee and I were listening to a Kid Capri mixtape. We were building on where we wanted to be in 10 years. By far, he was more informative than I was. I couldn't think past the next year for some reason. I

87

remember pausing in silence, then this premonition arose. In this I actually saw myself back in prison. I wasn't sure why I had this premonition at such a moment, however, I attribute it to the fact that it was my conscience convicting me for my actions. I dismissed it and snapped out of it.

My friend 'Da'mahna' pulled up with her best friend, chinky eyed 'Tayya', both were from the Parkside section of Camden. When I dismissed Tayya's request for me to come back over to her house, she cursed me out and said, "P@@sy...I hope they lock ya' ass up, fake ass hustler!" Then she pulled off. Lee and I laughed it off, and I just looked at it as wishful hating.

A half hour after this encounter while I was sitting comfortably in the car, I saw numerous of men charging towards me with guns drawn. As high and drunk as I was, I thought to raise the gun that I had under the seat and shoot, but these were not street dudes. They were detectives! Their chain-badges were a dead giveaway. They would have killed me if I would've processed my first thought.

"Dont fu**ing move! I'll blow your head off!" one of the detectives screamed.

As they removed us both from the car, I informed one of the detectives that Lee didn't have anything to do with this in an attempt to cut him loose and take the weight, but they took him anyway.

In the Camden police station, I thought about the premonition that I had right before this arrest. I told Lee about the premonition, and he was mad that I was just telling him about it.

The car we were in was a Porsche 911 that we had rented from a white guy from Cherry Hill, NJ. I had given him 10 bags of cocaine. Come to find out, his wife had called the police and reported the car stole. Go figure, right?

Of course my mother made it to the police station to pick me up embarrassed, disappointed, frustrated and hurt as usual! Complex within me was the seed of growth that this was just part of The Cost of operating in the streets.

88

I was asked a host of questions by 3 different detectives. Questions like, "What do I do to get the money that I had on me?" and "Was I a part of the Ninjas?" which was a huge car theft ring out of Camden in the 80's and 90's. They even questioned me about homicides, which of course I knew nothing about! That day I think I put out more "No's" then I ever did in my lifetime! It was unusual to be questioned in such a way for just a car reported missing and a gun found.

Truthfully my mind was not in tune with too much of what the police were talking about. I zeroed in on how they knew we were at the park. This was not a random street cop car type of bust. They mentioned numerous times that they had gotten a tip, and I had a great idea who this tipster was.

This was another frustrating experience that I had to muster up the strength to put behind me. After being lectured by my mother and being given a pinch of wisdom from my pops, I made a few phone calls, one to Portia and one to Lee, but Lee wasn't home.

In the backyard of our house we had a shed. I dug a hole in the back of it at the base and under the foundation. This is where I would stash all of my drugs and my gun. I learned my lesson from stashing my belongings in the house under my bed. A time when I got locked up my mother found bags of cocaine and my Pioneer house stereo system that I bought from a fiend stashed under the bed.

That night, I went around the block and continued to feed the drug habit of Amerikkka with an ambitious but nefarious foresight to make millions!!! I could smell it! I could feel it! I could taste it!

"You know you got fired, right?" my mother relayed. Hurt and pain filled her eyes running concurrently with watery frustration. She had just about enough, and I could see it! What could I say? No articulate excuse could justify my actions, and no form of apology could fix her heart as it was broken!

"Damn!!!!" I expressed to myself. "I fu**ed up!" I attempted to escape the terrible spirits left in the living room by escaping to the basement. I'd never seen my mother hurt and upset so deeply! Now I was in state of paralysis. This rare sense of inhumanity leveled my conscious reasoning.

My mother was my heart, and the Queen of my life!!! When my mother cried, I would cry all the while with her. It surely hurt me that she was hurt, and even more so because I was the cause of her pain!

In the basement I thought about my dreadful actions and the horrible life that I was leading thus far. Nothing I was doing was conducive to the plans that my family had for me. And at a very prolonging and painful Cost, they still loved me!!!

My pops had a bar in the basement. Time to time we would dip in and out of it. But on this day, I started going in on his Tangere. I ended up drinking myself to sleep and waking up late at night. I wiped the drool from the side of my mouth and arose to use the bathroom. I thought about going outside and transferring the pain I was feeling over to someone else, but instead I watched tv. I remember clear as day the HBO movie that came on. It starred the actor Gene Hackman and Roy Schneider called, "The French Connection". It was a 1940's type movie on French gangsters that dominated one of the busiest parts of the western Mediterranean and Marcelle's. I stayed up till after 4 in the morning watching that movie, intrigued by the monopoly they had going on. This movie had ranked up there with the movie "Scarface" and made an evil play on my psyche. I was so moved by this movie that I'd go on to do further research on it and found that a 1960 report showed that while narcotics agents were seizing about 200 pounds of heroin a year. The Carsican traffickers were smuggling in that amount per week. To me, this was the only sizable organized smuggling ring that was official then. In fact, this allowed the MOB to monopolize in the heroin trade from the 60's to the 70's.

I failed to process the inconceivable idea of what my mother was experiencing emotionally due in part to my involvement in criminal activities. However, I succeeded in processing the social construct, a poster to live up to totally disregarded of the positive "domesticconstruct" (home) that was before me.

Three days later, there was a family barbeque being held at my uncle and aunts house. Before this day, Sparty-Rock and I drove to New York early in the day. On the way up there, Bro was throwing all types of pitches to me. As I write, I call to mind the song on the Reasonable Doubt album by: Jay-Z where he said: "Ride wit' me I'll five you a G/ I'll ride wit' you for free/ I want the long-term riches and Bi***es..." Our conversation stretched from the smallest topics to the most personal. I was still reserved to my nature in trusting anyone. I'd become black-hearted. Sparty-Rock had me in Brooklyn, on East 56th St. I learned about official street legends like, Peewee Kirkland, Freddie Meyers, Frank Lucas and the likes. What kind of coincidence was this? Right after I watched that movie! Did I really need to witness this in my state of mind and weakened state of reality?

Bro drove to the Bronx and introduced me to some females on Grand Concourse, then to Sheraton Ave. We relaxed for a minute out there with a few dudes that he knew. That night we partied at the Tunnel, one of the hottest night clubs on the east coast. This was my first time going to the Tunnel, and good thing I had on clean socks, because before entering you had to take your shoes off and all types of other security procedures.

We parlayed in the Brooklyn section of the club. Every borough had their own section of the club. The females were willing and able, and I was too! This was life to me! The night didn't end until almost 6am with, and of course I found a lady to give me a "Happy Ending!"

Roslyn... Wow! Caught up in the mix of the lifestyle, I had been neglecting her. My cousin Lisette and I were real close. We understood each other, because we were the Black sheep's of the family in our own way. There was also my cousin 'Nate' who was a rebel as well.

Roslyn and I would barely see each other as crazy as it was, considering the immense love I had for her. Furthermore, we would only have sex like 3 times, and technically one of them was just an attempt. As a matter of fact,... It perplexes me visualizing how I would waste her time, emotions and trust on my complex lifestyle, thinking things would be splendid and normal like any woman expects in a relationship. I didn't respect the nature of her expectations at all! Selfishly and ignorantly, it wasn't about her nor us at all; it was about me! Adding on, the love I had for her was fraudulent. I was short of morals, values and standards that were needed to give love its meaning of truth. Roslyn's little sister 'Natalia', was my heart! She was! She would always instruct me to take care of her sister and treat her well, but unfortunately the both of them and their family fell victim to my disappointing actions. Doesn't that sound familiar?!? Wasn't my biologically family feeling the same exact way? And didn't they share the same atrocities? (SMH!)   July... weeks before my 17th birthday, I was pulling out of Woodbury's Bell Lake Apt. from a routine sexcapade with a female friend. Prior to this moment, earlier in the evening, what took place between me and my parents had literally reached its peak. I love my mother of course and my father, however, the feeling of stress, suffocation, misunderstanding and indignation began to overwhelm my soul! Logically speaking, I was being by the tail by my negative self-image. Approximately a little after 4am the police had pulled me over in Portia's Jeep (Isuzu Amigo). Well they tried to!!! In my indignant criminal behavioral ability, when I was alert on the red and blues, I quickly turned the corner, jumped out of the car and ran! As crazy as this is, in tote was my 9-millimeter handgun that I ended up discarding into some bushes. Just like always, I was caught though! How did I not see that this was going to be the outcome every time? I was like a dog chasing his tail, right? To no surprise at all, my attempts were quite visible to them. Technically, I was better seen throwing it than holding it! The officer informed me that he could've clearly shot me, considering his observation of the gun in my right hand, that had I not discarded it, there was an extreme possibility that I could've or would've been shot! This did not resonate. For my cognitive rights were smothered and inoperative due to such insidious empty dreams, hopes and expectations... What was I to do?!? Still, to me...it was "The Cost" of the game!!!!! without the presence of ingrowth moral standards that my tumultuous acts were clearly slowly and painfully Costing priceless gems, family and precious time!

CHAPTER VII

"MANAGING FAILURE!"

"The significant problems in life cannot be solved at the same level of thinking which created them!"

-Albert Einstein

Now back in juvenile detention, I began to zero in, striving to understand the depth of paternal love and force myself to reflect upon my role in not just family, but in society as a Black youth! I was intuitive enough to seek and know the concept of the world in its every day formula, but I was morally and spiritually bankrupt and not prepared to "understand" the concept of its complexities, and I surely was not willing to work as hard as my surrounding role models, had/have them working to reaching such kingship, in fact... truthfully... I lacked the feeling. I felt no real obligation to the wonderful gifts that I was blessed with from God and my parents. None!!!

Fact: By the age of 17, I knew how to cook, clean every spec of the house, wash clothes, fold clothes, iron clothes (correctly), fix & build things around the house, etc. This all came from the tutelage of my mother, step-father and biological father. I have always served as a humble, polite and respectful gentleman to my elders!

I now realize that back then my priorities were all misplaced, misconstrued and messed up! I was ego and pride driven. There were so many ways to exalt self to levels that I seen as prestigious, levels that actually cause infirmity in the structures of family and community, letters that are a cancer to a diminishing historical value. The devil had taken over the flesh of my being!

*****

"Norman...time to shackle up! Let's go!" the sheriff yelled. I was taking yet another slave ride to another slave camp. State#387872 awaits its owner. I was right back in Jamesburg's reception. Jamesburg reception was temporary housing until they classified you and assigned you to a plantation, where you would serve your time and obey your master while "he" capitalizes off of your involuntary servitude. Again, these are the managements that sustained my humanity and at such a shameful and painful Cost! Was I just a number? Or would I rise above this systemic oppressive number parallel to God's gift?!?

Depressingly, for imprisoned young and older men and women there lie many destructive elements that serve to eradicate one's ability to maintain or rather retain his or her humanity. I mean, just think...among us are many that remain to be disproportionately void of any mental, emotional and spiritual compassion. My bitter, angry, stressful confused and murderous third eye (mind) had so long ago lost such an authentic light, which once symbolized God's membership to the human race.

I was classified to remain at Jamesburg for the remainder of my sentence. I was given a year to run concurrent with my separate max out sentence for the gun charge that was pending. Cottage 10 was my slave quarters. This was the inductive indurated in a hell stricken environment. All the older young men or trouble makers/fighters resided here. Then I was truly convinced that I now had no chance of changing. These dudes offered not a bit of hope for that idea. I was where only the strong survive, and you had to have a negative type of strength in this setting.

I was greeted by "so-called" comrades that either did dirt with me on the streets or in jail at some point in my extensive criminal past. If you're an "official" dude you're always good for everything you need upon your initial arrival on the unit.

"Damn Bro! F**k you doin' back?"... "Yo, what happened my nigga?"... Are things that were said to me as I put my bag in room 23, which was a single cell.

I fell right back in the loop! In just weeks it was literally like I never even left! Phone calls to my parents, grandparents, Portia and Deasia were very expensive. Collect calls were nowhere near as cheap as they are today. Portia began to graciously support me with the few dollars I'd left at her house. She was 4 years older than I was, and she could handle responsibilities. Her career was a lucrative and stable one in Camden's City Hall. Clothes, pictures galore and mail was provided to me by her as well, along with a visit every other weekend. Roslyn was in Philly and had no way to initiate a visitation schedule. We would just constantly write back in forth and talk on the phone.

I retained the exact characteristics to establish Brotherhood on my compound with Brothers from Camden, Newark, Patterson, Jersey City, Elizabeth, etc... I was fly with everybody that was somebody, as being young men with influence, we all had some sort of common interests. As a matter of fact, I linked with just about 6 young men that I knew from Somerset Hills who were the new breed type of dudes, because their hearts had grown tremendously with immense destructive elements! They were the kill or plotting to kill type!

Truthfully, doing time transforms our youth into hateful boys in men's bodies! Their circumstances and invisibility create ignorance that grows from the seed of being ignored and not properly talked to. This forces the youths to build up their own intellect from ground zero. Therefore, they pick up ways, habits and intelligence from whatever influence they find, even if it's a bad one! While I'm struggling internally still asking myself questions in search of my identity like, "Who am I?"... "What am I?"... "Whom even cares?" Show me more!!! Love me and make me a provision for my confusion, not abandonment!

The provisions for a young man becomes only what he has been shown, taught, seen, inherited or heeded to throughout their upbringings. Being a human being and dealing with feelings and emotions gets you viewed as "weak" or "soft" and "not effective"! A place for loyalty is reserved for very few, depending on one's level of psychological and physiological common needs. However, even loyalty amongst that certain few is quickly shaken, and family easily becomes secondary and will serve no real purpose anymore.

We were allowed to watch tv), watching what was called a state movie, which was whatever VHS tape that the staff would bring in for us to watch. I made the conscious decision to remain outside and shoot the basketball around. My boy 'Lest' walked up, and we engaged in short conversation. From that short moment of politicking, we decided to escape! It was warm out, great weather for the month of September. The both of us were stressing and missing the streets hard! Portia had stopped supporting me the way that she was, stopped accepting my calls, kept what little bit of money that I had left and whatever other belongings that I left over her house. This was extremely stressful, because I had grown dependent on her support. Another thing that prison does is places you in a state of infancy, to where as though the most independent of men become dependent on someone or another. Now, I was planning to approach her for her act of unfaithfulness and betrayal. I could never retrieve a definitive explanation of why she committed such an act. I was good to this woman, mentally, emotionally and sexually, or so I thought I was. Was this The Cost of my disobedient, deceptive and manipulative behaviors?!? It is said that, God does not like ugly and is not too fond of the cute either! What isn't in His Will, will definitely be in his bill!

The next day, Lest and I met up near cottage 7, next to the football field, then disappeared into the woods. 200 yards away, we hid in a trailer that was equipped with a phone until it got dark out. We made all sorts of calls in between time. Of course we were caught only hours after our "Grand escape!" Not only was it too dark out, but it was a county that was densely populated with a bunch of wooded areas and barely any lights. The only thing Lest and I could think of was those old folk tales about the Jersey Devil. I myself, thought to just stand in the road and surrender! (lol!) This was in the total opposite way from the way I went the last time I escaped from here almost 2 years ago. Post apprehension, we were given 15 days in lock up and transferred to Epson (J.M.S.F). Well, I was... Lest was returned back to the compound due to the escape being his first attempt. I was given an extra year running concurrent with the sentence I already had. I would soon meet my fate though at The Cost of ignorance.

In the midst of the inflicting wounds that had fallen upon me, my mother, pops, sister, grandmother and grandfather, they were still willing and able to represent the hopefulness, beliefs, and love for me that they always had. Yet again, I was leaving my family stuck with disturbing the images of me. They were beginning to grow weaker due to my empty promises, plans, goals and endeavors that I had been pitching to them but failing to deliver on in the past.

Though I tried to go to school, get my G.E.D and learn something positive, unfortunately I just didn't have ambition nor the drive. My environment definitely wouldn't allow me to maintain a positive frame of mind. There was only one person that pushed me in a productive direction. He had 20 years to do, but he was a positive and humble dude that stayed to himself. The story on him was that he came in with a 5 year bid for an assault on his school teacher. However, at the end of his stay, he got into a fight with a kid and stabbed him to death, adding another 15 years onto his sentence. Whether the rumors were true or not, he was cool with me. He introduced me to the book Message to the Black Man by: Malcolm X. It helped that he was "God body" (Five Percent Nation) as I was as well. He had mastered 120, actual facts and solo facts (degrees of lessons that consisted of celestial and planets, etc.). I, on the other hand only mastered up to the 110-student enrollment. Still, even though we had a lot in common, I continued to embrace my cynical values and the more negative influences. I'd boxed the whole world in, especially considering what Portia, Roslyn, Spank and others had done! Bro, who I will call 'Mathematics', had been a forceful influence on my reflection of the tragic things I had done and the harm I had caused to my family. He would often share his personal stories of tragedy and wrong doing. To say the least, I was a choir boy compared to Bro! Man, his testimony was so impactful that in remembrance, I still till this day take the opportunity to contemplate and reflect on things that the brother verbalized to me pertaining to his thoughts and feelings in a general sense. He was a thorough

Brother! And he was from Asbury Park, also known as "Allah's Paradise" from its vast population of 5 percenters.

Surprisingly, I began to humble myself. I even enrolled back in school, voraciously attacking my work. Basketball was my thing. Nice wasn't a good enough comment for what I was on the court! I had Vince carter's ups back then! I could dunk any type of way and on anybody! J.M.S.F actually had an official basketball team with real uniforms and all. We played outside schools, programs, and even played Mercer County College. 2 specific games ended up being what could have been the catalyst of my success.

December 1990, we played Mercer County College. By halftime, I'd already scored 25 points, had 3 dunks, and the man I was guarding only held 4 points. We were all in the locker room when I got called out to meet the coach of the Mercer County College team that we were playing. To make a short story shorter, he was intrigued by my game and maturity with handling the ball. The plan was for me to remain in touch, contact him upon my release and he would take care of the rest.

I went in to finish the game with 38 points, 5 dunks and a host of assists. I had a chance to reconstruct my entire approach on life and finally work towards making something out of myself. My family would be proud of me as I made a historic redemption!

Mathematics pushed me, challenged me with constructive motive and called me out on my mistakes. It seemed as if the more we focused on studies and building, the more I would restrict myself from all the nonsense and violence that went on regularly. Even the level of conversation that were held in cyphers (verbal builds) with other brothers. The old things had begun to become distant from the belief system that I once possessed.

Roslyn's phone bill was $600. So it was cut off. I decided to make Deasia and a friend from Camden named 'Star' my rebound females. A sense of ingratitude fell upon me....

When I was 11 years old, I remember I pocketed a $50 bill from my pops dresser. My friends and I spent it all on candy! My pops came to me the next day and asked me if I took the money. Knowing my pops, it was in him to go back to his old ways and get a little gangster and whoop my ass! So I quickly said, "No sir!" My pops stooped down to my level as far as height, looked me in my revealing eyes to say, "Boy, you need to tell me the truth Jack! Say what you mean and mean what you say, because if you lie I'm tearing your little ass up!" My inner-voice to me to go ahead and tell the truth. "Yes, I took it..." My pops looked at me and smiled. "Boy, all a man's got is his word and his honor!"

*****

I was released once again May 17th, 1991. Instead of my mother picking me up, I insisted that the one of the counselors from J.M.S.F drop me off in Camden to my sister and her best friend.

I went against the natural common sense of God's plan. I was probably the goofiest, umbellic young dude in history with what I had done. Not feeling the idea of not having, I contacted SpartyRock ASAP! I guess I thought I was going to keep doing the same thing and get different results. I was literally insane!

My uncle attempted to slow me down and deter me from what I was trying to do. He didn't know much, but he knew I was up to no good from that sense of intuition that our wise elders have. Later that night, I was supposed to go back to Philly to pick up Roslyn and spend the night at the Holiday Inn on Roosevelt Blvd (The Boulevard) with her, but I ended up being rushed into Gloucester County Jail for a stolen Kawasaki Ninja 1100 motor cycle and a half ounce of cocaine.

Not even conscious moments of tense reflection could articulate this incognizant, unnatural stupidity that I harnessed as my own selfdestructive weaponry used against myself and the ones that love me the most! Perhaps I was an unfinished meal that needed more oven time, but at a Cost that was shadowed by stigmatic parasitized burdens!

I felt hurt and tormented from my inability to find a way to what I wanted, felt as though I needed and desired. What is it in me that is so empowering that it inflicts catastrophic pain and embarrassment, not only for myself, but my poor family! At 18 years old, I was feeling The Cost of all my idiotic behaviors deep enough to take this seriously! My family was emotionally weather-beaten and deeply affected to the core from my many malfunctions in society.

When I finally called my mother, she had already possessed that mother's intuition that something was wrong. The reason I gave for not coming straight home was annoying her! All she could say was, "Surprise to me...wow!" After getting off the phone with my moms, I laid on the bed in my holding cell from Friday to Monday. I may have eaten twice in the course of those 3 days.

My Step-pops was a sergeant at the time in Gloucester County Jail. Due to the conflict of interest I was shipped to Salem County Jail. Before my sad departure, my pops pulled me out of the holding cell to talk with me. I thought he was going to really let me have it verbally, but he came peacefully with great spiritual and general wisdom. "Look Jack, I'm not interested in what really happened. You're an adult now the rest is up to you..." Man, I couldn't even look him in his eyes! I was totally deflated! My self-esteem was low! Aside from being placed in another state of institutional dependence, I was also placed in an emotional state of distrust in myself! I should be a protector of my family!!!

I was back again, serving physical, mental, emotional and psychological time in an institution. Now, at 18 I felt like every bit of an old, grown soul. I spent exactly 6 months in Salem County Jail on a $75,000 cash bond.

The sad but funny thing about this is, out of all the individuals that I had ran with in the streets, only 3 attempted to post my bail. There was no assistance from anyone else. Sparty-Rock had given up $2,000, and there were lame excuses from everyone else. Most of these individuals I had either done dirt with or for, or helped out in some kind of way at some point in time. This showed me that friendship doesn't guarantee its use. Your "so called" Real Friends will leave you hanging.

*****

My step-pops had always been a mild-mannered Brother, a voice of reason even in chaotic situations. Despite the torment of the world that I placed myself in, he still made we aware that my divine place in the home still awaits me. He would say, "Boy, you...you got it. Daryl you're just not seeing it..."

More profound is that he and my mother deemed me worthy of and trusted me to insure their parenting was not in vein. I was feeling like I was forged in the fire of redemption! The wisdom from my parents and their attempts to awaken the man inside of me gave me hope within myself that I could be more than the person I saw myself to be. Truthfully, I was ugly inside! Spiritually I was bankrupt! I was inadequate, incompetent and angry.

For the first time in a long time I had a feeling of safety. Family is supposed to feel safe with each other, right? Isn't that what we always look for and expect to receive? Aren't we all looking for some safe haven where at all times we are in the presence of real friends or family? No one wants to have to keep looking over their shoulder. We know that our family has our best interest at heart and are conscious of our emotional and psychological safety. In that moment of created safety is the setting of stage, for so many amazing things and feelings are possible.

The coaching process of self is an ongoing journey in which I was the manager and the employee, constantly asking the right basic questions. I proposed to the positive pillars that stood with me to gain a better understanding of my purpose, my strengths, weaknesses, my opportunities for growth and development, hopes, fears and motives. I thought about all of the factors that would affect my ability to perform and reach my full potential. I needed to find out what God needed me to be! In me was a Special Seed!

Communication between my parents and I had strengthened. My sister Nae and I were always close, despite the fights we would have. What brother and sister doesn't fight? Regardless of whom or what, she was my everything and I always wanted to protect her, like a big brother is supposed to. I wanted to create that safe haven for her along with the rest of my sisters, brothers and family.

One evening, my mother and I engaged in an expressed dialogue that we never had before. I remember her asking what I really wanted to accomplish in life... Now, healthy relationships are usually not free of disagreement or conflict. However, if we always agree with each other there is no stimulus to get outside of ourselves and see things from other perspectives. I learned that the key is, when differences arise, we are not to judge, criticize or reject... In response to my mother asking what I wanted to accomplish in life was a shrug of my shoulders as if to say, "I don't know!" I knew I needed to produce more from my Black self than what stood present. But what?!? Normal parents may possibly have made a little light of the situation at hand, but normality was not documented in my mother's psyche. The shrug of my shoulders fell on deaf ears as my mother did not want to hear that response. This angered her extravagantly.

Historically thinking, the innate drive, ambition and ability of my mother and step-father warranted nothing short of progress. This, I believe with respect to both of their own personal lineage and their being born in the 50's when the Black population had less than equal standing as opposed to whites. They were born struggling for equality and witnessed violence directed at Black people all over Amerikkka. So any possible judgment or criticism passed down from such a profound historical place was ingested.

In order to reconstruct, I had to reconsider the heart of my lineage. If I am to speak of repair, it will take much to repair from the damage that the former slave masters and their children have done to Black people (and other minorities) in Amerikkka. No wonder the apostle
Paul said in truth, "Be ye not conformed to this world, but be ye transformed by the renewing of your mind!" However, I could not

103

renew my mind until I uprooted the ideas that ruled my mind and replaced it with the ideas of Black Nationalism.

*****

February 1992, in a broken counterclockwise circle, my feet just as equal in mind danced around the truth of life long enough to become a root cause to hinder the efforts of myself from adhering to my parents hearts. My blind disobedience seemed to always be the 10 ton gorilla on my back, and I think I seemed to like it. When will it end? At what Cost will this bill of deprivation finally add up to? Life in prison? Death? Homelessness? Please connect me to my historical roots! I can't seem to find my way!

I still had to face the charges that I had incurred a year ago. The courts were offering me 5 years for both the stolen motor cycle and the gun. Hell no! I wasn't signing that plea agreement!

Remember the $2,000 that Sparty-Rock put towards my bail? I used it for the purpose of retaining a real lawyer, but the court appointed public defenders are so inundated with cases that it's difficult to receive the adequate representation from them.

For some reason, being broke always seemed to enlighten me in many ways, one way being in humility. I guess the humility comes from the fact that life shows up with its complexities when you're broke. You tell me? But I wasn't the one to just sit around, do nothing and accept being broke! Furthermore, the devil had assassinated my happiness, stole my peace and destroyed my home.

Doe was locked-up for being caught with 30 pounds of weed in Jersey and was fighting his case. The block was open, and there was a new breed of hustlers making names for themselves. The game had gone from $20 bags to dime ($10) bags. A lot had changed in the streets. I knew this from keeping my ear close to the mouths of those who were in them.

I was a huge partaker in the party scene, from the Ritz, Gotham Nightclub, Club Vegas in Philly, Rick Mohorne's in Cherry Hill, Sensations in Newark, NJ, to clubs in Atlanta and New York. I would sit in the house and literally stress, contemplating what I needed to do next. This revealed many blind spots in me, the things I could not see. Getting me to believe in change was one difference, but getting me to actually change was another. A woman by the name of Sharonda that I was messing with tried her best to give an impressionable account as to why I needed to refrain from the streets and the night life and instead concentrate on a more moral and spiritual life. However, as correct as she stood in her approach, I wasn't trying to hear it.

Sharonda was 5'6, about 125 lbs., caramel skin tone with these alluring green eyes and a petite thickness just like them. She was mild mannered and well read. I met her through my 'S'. He was messing with her cousin, and we just so happened to bump into each other.

At the time, my heart knew that I needed work in many areas of my life, but there were no agreeable facts about the severity of my problems. Never did I stop to fully think or understand the impact of my behaviors. I went back to what "I thought" I knew best!

*****

Sharonda and I departed from my attorney's office one afternoon and stopped to eat. As we dug into our meals, she witnessed the look of aggravation written on my face. (I can actually remember now exactly how I was feeling then. It was that intense!) My eyebrows were so scrunched up that it gave me a painful headache.

"Are you alright Bae?" she asked.

"Hell no!" I replied, shaking my head no.

She then went on to open up a floodgate of wisdom pertaining to my ongoing situation. I wasn't prepared to face trial for the charges that I had pending, especially knowing that if I was found guilty I was facing 20 years in prison. The more I discussed this reality with her, the more the psychological effects of the weed needed to be addressed. So I pardoned myself from the table, went outside to the car, rolled up and smoked real quick. I thought about just going on the run, just getting away from all of this discordant drama, but I couldn't. I created it all, and I had to face and fix it!

How you walk, how you greet people, how you dress, even how you drink; everything you do and say speaks on how people perceive you. And this was my main platform. Whether you love me, like me, or respected me... hated me, dislike me, feared me, or didn't respect me, you knew me! It just so happens that, the brother I was speaking to this specific day took a liking to me many years prior to this moment and had some encouraging words for me. He was a friend of my pops that worked for the sheriff's department named 'Ebron'. Every time I saw him he always had something positive to say, which meant nothing to me then, but means everything to me in my hindsight.

February 2nd, 1992, the first day of trial, I was accompanied by Sharonda, her sister, S, Lee, and my attorney. The long and emotionally arduous wait was now coming full circle. Sitting out in the waiting area felt like I was awaiting a firing squad! Readily to determine my fate, I recall in periodic fashion glancing to the right, in hopes that my mother would walk through the double doors to support her son as his life lie in the bounds of 13 strangers (12 jurors and the judge). The internal cries were real!!! The rotting inside! The loneliness! I was feeling all of this despite the friends sitting next to me in support. Knowing that if the court sealed my envelope and mailed me to the slave camp that I would be just another invisible Black man... Out of sight, out of mind!!! But family... well, they'll always know you, see and love you for who you are and desire that you soar above the temptations of the world. For my family themselves persisted to motivate me to grab and embrace my greatest potentials!

"Docket number w-410433-0822, on the 3-count indictment..." I heard the court clerk yell for all in the courtroom to hear. I was in a daydream. It seemed like the voice of my loved ones were paramount in my head.

That first morning in court, the selection and swearing in of the jury took place. All of the pending pretrial motions were disposed of and the opening statements were presented. The state went first, providing their accounts. Then my attorney provided the jury and the court with his prospective and called forth a witness of ours. I remember glancing back at those who came to support me. All the while I was sitting in that seat with an innate feeling like my body was having a celestial outer body experience. I was startled out of this state by the court announcing that they were adjourning the proceedings until the afternoon. We walked across the street to eat at the courthouse cafe, a spot where lawyers, judges, prosecutors, etc. to eat.

Court was back in session! It began with a testimony from a detective from Woodbury PD. We had to listen to this "so called" public servant fabricate stories and evidence, deceiving the court. It sounded true until my attorney dug into his mountain of lies. I was confident and comforted by my attorney's cross examination, pointing out the detective's inconsistencies compared to the facts in my attorney's report.

In 3 days, a total of 3 detectives and a uniformed police officer testified with lying tongues. However, one by one, my attorney exposed them. He had advised me that the state's case was weak and both sides prepared for closing arguments.

The last day of trial, when both sides had finished their closing arguments, the judge began the instructions of the jury. This process was so long and boring that I began to fall asleep. I never really pondered how imperative that hour and half process was to my liberty or what would happen if the instructions happened to be erroneous. All I knew was that I put the money out for a good lawyer, and I needed to walk out of here without handcuffs on. In retrospect, I still thought life was a game, that anything short of my release didn't matter. After the jury instructions, the jury went back to deliberate and decide on my fate.

As Sharonda, her sister, S and I spilled out in the hallway, I went to the payphones to make a phone call.

"Hardcourt, Brace and Javonevich, how may I help you?"

"Good afternoon! May I speak to P.V. please?" I asked.

"Oh! Hi Daryl! I will connect you."

"Thank you..." I waited.

"Hello, P.V. speaking."

"Mom!" This dialogue again created an outer body experience. I knew I had compromised my integrity and that of a generational blessing. My grandparents and parents worked too hard, sacrificed their own dreams, wants and desires so that I could better use my gifts and talents. They always prayed for me and with me even! In this bit of wisdom my mother spoke through the phone, she emphasized that I was grown now, and I needed to figure it out. She was tired of this trip down this emotional road I traveled, and I couldn't even blame her. This was all on me.

As I was sitting with my attorney, my heart was beating out of my chest. Sharonda had laid her head on my shoulder as she spoke to me. The combination of her words and my mother's words bounced around in my head like a pinball!

The bailiff called us in. I locked eyes with 2 of the "public servants" (detectives). Those with me were staring into the deceptive eyes of these people as well. I walked in with the semblance of a smirk on my face aimed towards them, but my 2 feet actually didn't want to travel that deciding 10 miles it seemed to walk. I took my seat as we awaited the judge's arrival. Soon after, the jury filed back into the courtroom. I glanced back as I heard the doors to the courtroom open. It was Lee, Fat-Joe, and some random female. I gave them a head nod and a huge smile. Turning back around, I was supernervous! I did some small-talk with my attorney while awaiting my fate. Despite my nerves, a sense of comfort dropped upon me knowing my peoples were behind me in this battle. But still, I was feeling some type of way that it wasn't my moms or pops, my sister, grandparents, or any other family members.

108

"All rise!" the bailiff roared to the courts. My legs were feeble in my standing. When we sat back down, I almost hyperventilated in that courtroom.

"Have you, the jury reached a verdict?" the judge asked the jury.

"Yes, your honor!" one of the jurors replied.

I was having yet another outer body experience. I began to reminisce about all the things that I had done to pave the road leading to this ugly place that I was now in. Was this, in return, The Cost of me doing numbers out in the streets? The money I made! The number of women I dealt with! The amount of "so called" friends I had! The time I had done! The steps I took! The family that I hurt! The people that I harmed! Was it all worth what I was going through at this present moment? I was about to be judged by 8 white people, 4 Blacks and an overrated white man in a black robe that had not a clue who "the real" Daryl M. Norman was!

"...On count one of the indictment, what say you?" the judge spoke to the jurors.

"Not guilty!" the juror stated as I let out a sigh of relief and my supporters clapped their hands in excitement. I still had 2 more indictments to go though.

"On count two of the indictment, what say you?"

"Not Guilty!" I took a deep breath and looked up at the ceiling shaking my head.

"Count three on the indictment, what say you?" I took a deep breath and held it in as my heart was beating like a drum.

"Not guilty your honor!" I closed my eyes, shook my head and thanked God!

Immediately after, I called my mother to relay the good news. Then, I called my grandparents. I asked my grandfather to pick me up from the courthouse in Woodbury. My grandparents lived in

Deptford, in the Jerico section, just 5 minutes away from where I was.

Everybody was celebrating, but I was humbled by this. I explained to them that I needed to go to my family's house for a few hours and that I would meet them at Sharonda's house.

As far back as I can remember, my grandparents had always been my greatest buddies and everything you want in a grandparent. Even when I screwed up (which was regular for me), they were still there for me, praying for me! In them, there was not a micro-spec of betrayal or judgment!

My grandmother was very serious in her relationship with God! She was blessed, highly favored and stood out as a remarkable example of God's gift to humanity! I can recall one scripture from the Bible that she made me fond of, Isaiah (40:29-31): "He gives power to the weak, and to those who have no might He increases strength. Even the youths shall faint and be weary, and the young men shall utterly fall, but those who wait on the Lord shall mount up with wings like eagles, they shall run and not be weary, they shall walk and not faint." Yeah, my grandmother was a spiritual gift to this world!

My grandfather always embraced me as his son! He would address me as "Son"! Granted that, sometimes he would get a little excited. When he would call me, he would get stuck saying all of my uncle names before getting my name right. he would be like, "Uhhh...you, you know who I'm talking to..." or he would just say, "Come here Boy!" (lol!) My grandparents were the best!

For 6 hours, we spoke, cried, ate, laughed and prayed. I was not very spiritual or religious at the time, but I felt an honest peace over me and in me. This was my safe haven, where I belonged. This was my refuge from the world and its troubles as well...

*****

In the spring of 1992, I was consumed by the tumultuous effects of the devil's temptations. Hammered with the winds of instability, I made a perverse judgment and returned to the streets.

By this time, my family's intuition had already served them their worst concern, who I was! You know the saying, "You can fool some people some of the time, but you can't fool some people all of the time!" My eyes didn't match my smile and in my twisted pathology, no one could see me. However, my loved ones could. They saw right through all of my lies and deception! They allowed me to walk this plank by my lonesome, and if I fell... well, I had to just brace myself for a hard landing!

They say, "If you fail to plan, then you plan to fail!" And without a roadmap or navigation system you will get lost through life. Every plan starts with a vision, then blueprints get formulated, then execution! It's not enough to have a plan though! You have to work at that plan until you succeed.

Most people (like myself) don't see their plans out to the end. If something is not working, or if it's not happening fast enough, we abandon everything!

That is not the way though! You have to be persistent with your plans. If it fails, come up with another approach and keep at it until you succeed. You learn from your mistakes and the things that don't go right. Quitters never win, and winners never quit!

CHAPTER VIII

TRUTHS & DARES

Out of all the things in the world, history is the only thing that can record a man's life! I thought to myself, what is the point of living if no one remembers that you were here? If you do something, do the damn thing! Do it big or don't do it at all! When you check out, make sure they remember your name. Make sure enough was done, more good than bad!

*****

It was July 30th, on a Friday, and I was now 20 years old. It was lady's night at the 1048 Club. My lady friend and 5 of her girls were down from New York. I had met this lady friend in Miami a few months back. We partied heavy, drank good and smoked a few blunts together.

Mando asked if we were going to "The Whip" (an after-hour club). Him and K were leaving as the club was letting out. Lee and Tee were trying to hurry me up. I had my car double-parked, system dumping, playing the Das Effects CD. My lady friend and her girls were behind my car. I went to my car and let my lady friend in the passenger seat. I shut the door, and before I got around to the driver's side, here comes one of my other lady friends, 'Jaleese', walking my way, screaming frantically, "Who is that? Who is she? What you doin'? Hell no!" I got in the car and pulled off.

Jaleese happened to be my new acquaintance. Actually we had been real close friends if you know what I mean! She was 7 years older than I was with kids, and she was a great mother. She was a petite 5'2, light skinned, gorgeous woman! The relationship was astringent for the both of us. It was all just physical attraction and great sex. The both of us were just kids at heart. I was up and winning, and my moral gauge was definitely questionable.

Now that things began to pick up for me, the money I made grew on me like it was my hair. The seed was planted, watered and nourished from the root to the sky, and my desires, wants, needs and expectations grew with it as well. Some nights I would find myself internally haunted by this new lifestyle, but I was powerless now to stop it and the drama that came with it!

It was August 27th, the day of Jaleesa's 28th birthday. I was loving enough to secure the firehouse for her party, drinks, food, etc. When you are counted on for fully supporting your mate, things like that are expected of you. Not for me though! When my behind was supposed to be in the house showering and dressing, my greed had my mind racing and running around on street hours. This indeed could have waited till perhaps the next day. However, there were other hustlers selling bags with my stamp on them, but with their cocaine in it. Truthfully... these dudes not only put the battery in my back, but they kicked it in! Lee had pulled up in front of the house and hit the horn. I was actually ignoring Lee too, but that was my homie. In my heart, loyalty is love, so I answered his call of concern. Jaleesa was about to leave with 2 of her friends and get dressed over her girlfriend's house. She asked, "You going out to see what that fool want?" Of course her outlook on my company didn't matter to me. Sitting in his car, Lee spilled the news that Dee, this dude named 'Choc' and his OT (out of town) boys were out on Delaware St. Now, we had been having this issue with these dudes all summer just about. My cousin and I approached Dee on a few occasions considering the fact that this town wasn't big enough for all these other dudes. Plus, my stamp was on their bags; which he denied. Jaleesa and her girls got in her car as she leaned in and kissed me goodbye and told me to hurry up. I locked the doors to the house, got in the car and rode 2 blocks over to my man 'Puma's' house. 3 of my closest comrades Iggy, Bill-Blast and Snoop all joined me as I walked around to Delaware St. where Dee, Choc and their OT company were at. This of course was the catalyst for a huge physical battle, which we got the best of them in. But in the midst of my confrontation with one of the dudes, my gun fell out of my waist, and one of them tried to pick it, in which he failed in his efforts. Whatever money that they had, chain, watch or new sneakers was taken from them! This was not only an intricate move to provoke and test these dude's street cred, but a plea to the hood that loyalty is everything! And through it all I was riding! John C. Maxwell said, "Great leaders rarely think in terms of boundaries; they think in terms of opportunities!"

When someone like myself reasons dichotomously, or uses what is called either or thinking, I tend to see individuals or situations as being all good or all bad. I will not look in the area in between which could sometimes put a different or more reasonable light on the problem. For example: if I think dichotomously, I might look at things as if all problems are caused by external factors, or other people, or circumstances beyond my control. This type of thinking leads me to imagining that criticism from external beings means I'm not living up to "keeping it real" or I'm just outright misunderstood!

By chance, I took this opportunity to inject my ideology in the individual standing in attendance as we laughed about what happened in front of Iggy's house, and amazingly this all took place in an hour followed by what happened next. We all dispersed and went our separate ways. Snoop and I walked up Adams street, talking about the party, etc. We got to Washington and Spruce St, and a car full of dudes pulled up, tires screeching. I knew right from the jump that this was probably my actions pulling up to give back what I dished out! They were like clowns in a circus car piling out on me. I directed Snoop to go in the house since he didn't have a gun in case a melee of gunfire broke out. In a backwards retreat, I attempted to get distance. I had looked down on their bats and 2x4's and tried to pull out the 9mm from my pocket which kept getting stuck. I guess not knowing I had the gun on me they kept coming at me, and I accidently let the gun off through my pants pocket. Surprisingly, they kept coming after me. My leg was burning from the heat of the muzzle being so close to my leg. I finally got the gun out of my pocket and sent the first 2 shots directly at them with malicious intent. All of them quickly did a 180 and ran, some went back to the car and some abandoned the vehicle. As they pulled off, I let 4 more shots off at the car. This melodramatic script had been deemed improvident. But after the fact, my inchoative thought was that Dee and Cho were not built for this dramaturgic stage play. In

114

all reality, I was not either. Introspect, I had known Dee to tell. He had told on his man Asap from the Bronx, NY. Asap came looking for Dee, because Dee owed him some money for a quarter bird that he fronted him. While he was in the town looking for Dee, I ran into dude, and he spilled the news to me about Dee telling on his mans in New York.

In our culture, there seems to always be an underlying premise or assumption that as people, even those of diverse ethnicities, tend to remain in competition which brews counterproductive conflicts, hostility and anger. Problematically, next is a term of our individualistic conceptions of who we are, rather than who we are in Unity, as a whole, as a people! Are we the only race of people that is in anguish over the question, who am I? That question arises in part from a lack of education at village teaching, also the rush of an industrial society that marginalized us in such diverse and strategic ways when emancipated from the south so long ago! Whatever the cause, historical truth provides a broader context of our Black identity and the dilemmas that stand in our way until this day.

In the proof of my actions existed a strong sense of what I would do in order to protect who I am and what I was doing. Followed by that was the police showing up at my house. "Damn!" was my reaction as I grabbed my money, keys and gun and ran out the back door. I had Snoop with me. The 2 of us hit fence after fence until we were until we were far enough away from the raid of my house. I offered Snoop an apology for the misfortune, which went void due to his loyalty to the streets. Oddly, this was normal to us!

Detectives happened to raid every spot that I was known to frequent looking for me, including my parents house. They were upset, but they were far from surprised. My parents loved me and prayed for me on the regular, however, it was my life, and they were allowing me to nurture and cultivate my own character and personality in the world. I was in my own world though, a world that seemed to be emotionally weather-beaten. How long could I really bear to carry this weight on my back with an impression that all was well when it wasn't? In the shadow of the life I was living lie truth of a perdurable community of others, family! I had dreaded this other life though! Even those that I thought to have cared about shook my hand in solidarity and truthfully shook my trust! Yet, I had earned this!!! What did I expect from strangers?

I insisted on being "in the loop" (the swing of things). I was suffering from a tangent impurity. The world I created started to box me in more and more on a psychological level. The plans had gone amiss that my parents and grandparents had high and genuine hopes for me to fulfill--the plans that God had for me! However, my heart was Black and full of ugly and animal-like qualities! I was displaying unrelenting portrayals of self-imagery, of being The Cost. Culturally I was moving backward! I was primitively and intellectually stunted! Because of this, I was prone to violence! I was morally corrupted! I was spiritually bankrupt!!!

Visits to my mothers were of a regularity for me. I still attended some family functions. You know, like cook-outs and occasional visits to see my grandparents. My grandfather was very enlightening. This man knew the Bible from cover to cover. He would immerse me in his wisdom. Those soothing and soul piercing words would always seat me in sort of a trance. His prudence as a Black family man was amazing!

My conscience would emerge whenever I was made party to this positive construct, causing me to feel a bit guilty of my daily actions as a Black man and a an offspring of the Spencer family tree. In all actuality, I was a disgrace to my family!

The world view on and statistical stigma held against the Black youth is damaging to the psyche. What our youths are made to believe is that there are limitations and outside of the "concrete jungle" (the hood) is out of bounds. To me, the lifestyle opposite of mine and my constituents was foreign!

My grandparents always dispelled these myths though! They extended so much accurate wisdom towards selfless service and motivations toward humanity. The sad part is, I was a fool! And fools don't heed wisdom!

*****

On September 8th 1992, I was picked up by police and arrested for the incident involving Dee and his cronies. I was charged with unlawful possession of a weapon (handgun), in lawful purpose firearms, criminal attempt, hindering apprehension, aggravated menacing, etc, etc... My bail ended up being $150,000, cash only!

Another trip to a receptional slave camp, proving the statistics to be accurate! This was also another notch of embarrassment for my family. However, I didn't feel too embarrassed. I guess my intrinsic values began to assimilate to this norm--a regulative seat in the undermining factor of who and what I am and where I need to be in life as a man!

This unfortunate situation turned out to be more less fortunate. It was a blessing in disguise! Despite the fact that Dee had his girlfriend call the police on me, they didn't want to pursue with the charges nor testify against me. The state also didn't offer to pick the charges up and prosecute.

Not once did I stop to try and understand the seriousness of my failures. I had not one dreadful reminder of the horrors that stifled my life and suffocated others! It seemed as if this cold and ruthless heart was conflicted with a half heart of compassion. I mean... I don't think I was ever an insane or insidious person. In fact, within me existed a room of great mannerisms, kindness and a bit of integrity, especially towards my elders! However, I was confined to this inability to release what lived inside of me. It was difficult to get from under this impoverished weight that was bestowed upon me. There was so much potential in my intellect, spirit and flesh, but I didn't see it! I didn't see what everyone of sound mind around me was seeing, the Greatness in me! But low and behold, it was always there!

Many of times I would drive to Fairmount Park alone, drink my Hennessey and smoke excessive amount of weed to the face! I was an old school music head! So I would ease back and mellow out to the sounds of Luther Vandross. Moments of continual stress had begun to encompass my fate. My unstable life was the sentence that I was given. I wanted, needed and desired to be better, but I was weak! I was suffering from the absence of "the voice of reason"! However, the presence of the voice of self-doubt continued to reign over me.

I remember asking certain people about fatherhood, mainly my step-pops and my biological father. Firsthand, I observed an example of a blessed, selfless Christian love that my step pops had for my mother.

*****

In August of 1993, I met 'Kiah'. We were immediately drawn to one another. She was from a sort of a big family in Paulsboro, NJ. Kiah was quiet, a natural beauty, didn't wear any make-up, and she had a nice, petite body. Just the way that she walked captivated my attention!

I was dead wrong for engaging in a second of mindful lust over her, but I lacked control, self-love and respect. To consummate our expression of interest and lust, we started having sex regularly.

I'd be remiss if I failed to expound on the effects of my decisions pertaining to Kiah. To my excitement nervousness, the revelation manifested of her being pregnant. It put me on a defense when I should've been a proud man. She was excited. Her personality joyously illuminated the open space of the community, but I was incapable of initiating the reciprocal dynamic required to consummate her expression of love. In fact, I made a terrible response, something to the same effect of, "Is it mine?"

I was sure as to how I would tell Jaleese. My actions continued to disrupt a life of trust with the equal opposite, distrust. As Jaleese asked me about Kiah's pregnancy, I was not shocked that she found out. I should've been man enough to be the one to tell her. She called me every name in the book of anger and kicked me out.

I took care of Kiah as much as I was able to. Considering that she was carrying my child and she was a good girl, her family wasn't happy with the situation.

Four months into her pregnancy, I got locked up for distribution of cocaine, possession of CDS, possession of CDS with intent to distribute and employing a juvenile in a drug distribution scheme.

As the sun began to set on my journeys, I was now back to square one. Nothing I had accomplished in the streets meant anything. Partying, all the women from town to town and state to state and excessive money spent on clothes and shoes, it was all over. I was basically broke.

Jaleese and my friend from North Philly as well as Lee contacted a bail bondsman in Elizabeth, NJ, in which they were able to negotiate with them. They each gave the bail bondsmen $2,000 for a $75,000 bail.

Being broke was synonymous to a death sentence for me. I had a child on the way, so I disregarded the foreseen consequences for my actions and got right back to it! I started putting my new gun to use My first 2 jouxes (robberies) went without a fight of course. I knew I needed a bigger come up. However, with a bigger take comes a bigger gun!

An associate of mine provided me with a Mac-10 submachine gun! He even made me aware that the gun was "dirty" (had been used in a crime). That would steer a man who thought critically about things away, but I guess I wasn't a critical thinker, because I took it with honor, even knowing if I got caught with it I would more than likely be facing charges for something I didn't do! How foolish of me, right?

My brother 'Rod' and I would drink together and kick it. He'd be forthright in comparing me with my biological father, because my father had overcome some challenges as well. Like any other Black man born in the 50's, he wasn't trying to get over; he was just trying to survive the 70's...

*****

April of 1994, I was incarcerated yet again! This time I was given 5 years in state prison. However, my attorney, through his experience, forced the courts to resentence me to a 3 year term instead.

Kiah had my son, 'Day'Quan Lashawn Norman Wallace', on May 28, 1994. I was ever so elated! I was blessed with photos of my son, and I immediately began to have an epiphany. Kiah and Day'Quan would need me to man up and be responsible. I began to question if I were a true friend and companion to Kiah. Could I be? or would I be?

As I have shared numerously, I was not the good or the greatest man or completely cognizant in my identity. I must also concede that I was not always true to my word!

Initially, from the day of my confinement there were conscious efforts to seek the truth of who I am, what I wanted to do with my life, I started working on staying true to my word. I'd lied to and upset my family enough with all the empty promises. Before leaving the Gloucester County Jail, my step-pop told me, "I know you got it in you, get it together Jack! I'll se you when you get back..."

Sitting and awaiting my departure from Yardville Youth Correctional Facility's reception unit, I was classified to Bordentown a.k.a Gladiator School.

One day, as I was sitting inside my cell reading the Bible, I thought about a scripture that my grandfather directed me to in the book of Jeremiah. I began to read, pray and talk to God. I even remembered the premonition that I had years ago about seeing myself in prison. Reading the Bible started to perplex me. I attempted to rationalize my behaviors and decisions.

I'd say, I left 2 lives (my son and his mother) in such an unbalanced world without respect to their individual needs! Though I was arrested, to be totally truthful, prior to my arrest, I was not so much actively involved in the full help of nurturing my son and should

120

have been so much more to Kiah! In all realness, I had left Kiah and my son long before he was born!

I spent the remainder of my eighteen months in Bordentown. In between my stay, given the fact of Bordentown being Gladiator School, I'd luckily only managed to get into 5 fights. Prisons don't have an invested interest in our wellbeing; only on invested financial interest in the wellbeing in the occupancy of the institutions.

Many of our Black youths are suffering the consequences of the oppressive and mean-spirited policies white Amerikkka imposes regularly. There is a lack of structural policies that afford the youth the proper emotional and psychological assistance needed. We have been descendants of men and women whose spirits were broken by these same exact practices for generations.

When Kiah and Day'Quan would visit me, it brought a great restoration. I was a very proud father! I loved my son like no other father could! I felt as though the love I had for my son was truly beyond the norm, which called to my own father's love, both my biological father and step-father. How could I accept this responsibility fully when I was released?

All of the children that are deprived of the love and comfort of parents, lost to prison, drugs or the streets. I saw and still see the magnitude of disappointment that plagues these deprived children, men, women and communities from the unanswered call for fatherhood.

How was I to embrace these truth of, not only parenthood, but manhood? when in all actuality the double-mindedness continued to eradicate the historical nature of truth. I was still just a number.

121

EPISODIC NATURES

"A man against his own will is of the same opinion still!"

February 26, 1996, my mother and pops were right out front of Bordentown to greet me. Considering the gall dynamics of all that I had put them through over the years, their love still fortified the conclusion that they were my best of friends and offered more solace than one could ever imagine. With a stern embrace as if I were just born, they hugged me close and welcomed my release.

Returning back home to my parent's house gave me an awkward, but vigorous feeling as soon as we pulled up. Guess who was at the door awaiting my arrival? Day'Quan! It was like he had this premonition himself. He was now 2 years old. I recall him being very inquisitive, attentive and having a great memory. At 2 years old, even though there was no clarity in his wording of things, he would tap me, then point and try his best to say whatever it was that he was asking for or about.

My son and I were inseparable! Everything a father was expected to do was done!

The reality of life showed up and legitimately decimated my ability to maintain. I was just as uncoordinated as I was before I did that time. However, I did acquire another level to the standard of selfawareness and social intelligence. I was still manipulating my way through life.

My face experienced more doors slammed on it, than a door to door salesman. No jobs were hiring, and my son needed the essentials that every child needs. Therefore, I needed the outlet to make ends meet. So it was back to what "I thought" I knew best!

I was very impulsive! I was full of pride! And I was believed to have been a bit psychosomatic! This led to a parole violation, which led to a warrant being issued for my arrest, which then turned into me running from parole and staying in Delaware. Of course I upset and disappointed my family members.

My son's birthday was the 28th of May, which landed on a Tuesday. We planned his birthday party at Chuck E. Cheese for the following weekend. 2 weeks prior to his birthday, me and 10 of my closest associates went to Miami for a week, then went straight to Virginia Beach where we stayed for 4 days. Then we went to D.C. for Memorial Day Weekend. I knew I was going back behind bars eventually, so I partied hard, probably harder than I ever did in my life!

I told my parents and Kiah that I would turn myself in after Day'Quan's party. That never happened though, because on June 8th, I was randomly stopped by Camden Police for a routine traffic stop. Instead of lying about my situation, I let them know that I had a warrant for a parole violation. I think that was the most honest thing that I had ever done thus far.

I was released from Camden County Jail on September 6, 1996. I had maxed out, so I had no parole! Even in just those couple of months I was gone things changed.

By this time, most of the individuals that I knew, hustled with or partied with were either murdered or in jail! There was also a presence of those few that fell victim to sniffing heroin and became a shell of what they used to be. The last thing I wanted was to become like the many that I once ran with. But what I had become was no different than any drug abuser. I may have attempted to intellectualize the "keeping it real" street vernacular with noisy rhetoric, but reality says, "This is a disease!" I was living in and out of the streets committing an enjoyed amount of crimes. How do I cure this motion sickness? Because naturally, if in fact I was cognizant from a sobrietal state while I was doing the things that I was doing, I wouldn't have been sickened with cognitive unreasoning.

I continued in my oppressive suppression and criminal activities without post thoughts of my past! Before moving forward, allow me to say this:

Cocaine was first used in the late 1800's and early 1900's before its dangers were actually recognized. It was used by doctors as an anesthetic, because of its effectiveness. It also causes a short-lived euphoria, suppresses the appetite, interferes with sleep and increases the heart rate and blood pressure. Furthermore, cocaine has also been linked to heart attacks and cerebral hemorrhages. Repeated usage is required to maintain a "high", and abusers who try to abstain often experience a tremendous craving for the drug--a hallmark of addiction.

Clearly this sounds indicative to the dependencies and symptoms of a "normal street hustler" as I was. Short-lived euphoria tends to materialize; the existence of and the absence from beautiful women, sex money, clothes, cars, jewelry, and even gunplay! The streets also cause a suppression of appetite. and interferes with our sleep. This social economical circumference pressures us to protect ourselves from the hands of the corrupt police, the broken criminal justice system, and the diseased minds of individuals that perhaps want to harm you for whatever reason.

Despite these facts, I still returned to the streets full force, hustling and striving to attain these past intriguing visions. Reiterating what K-Bang said in Lost Souls (Part 1), this was me:

"Wasting time. Chasing social recognition. Scattered thinking!

Compulsive lying. Excessive drug use and excessive drinking!

Lost Souls are extremely emotional creatures that make rash decisions!

Most of them are have reached adulthood, but are still very much in need of some sort of supervision..."

My man S.D. and I had allocated a few dollars, investing in a car and truck detailing service on Carmen St., in Camden, NJ. In all truth, this was just a front for buying and selling stolen vehicles. We would pay younger individuals $200-$500 to steal the cars, then refer to a ledger. We would pay this certain person and somehow the vin numbers on every car would read new, ready to be legal and registered. Depending on the make, model and year of the car, they would be sold anywhere from 15 to $20,000!

I was hell-bent on proving my status in the streets with an audacious and renewed hope. This time around, my internal feelings were different! On the other hand, it seemed as if everyone in my family had a semblance of hope in pursuing their goals, dreams and endeavors. Either they were educating themselves, buying or preparing to buy a house, or doing other productive things in life. From where I stood was a nightmare in a field of the darkest cold.

"I've been wasting potential for years in these streets. If I can look forward to the opportunity to put up at least half a million dollars, I promise to square up like a pool table!" I remember saying this to Aliah and S.D.

Aliah had a hand in Quail Run Apartments, in Lindenwold, NJ, selling cocaine. This relationship was disastrous! But if you let me tell it, it was great! We enjoyed each other in every way possible, but along with her came a lot of inherited drama that contributed to my fall! Actually, my initial decision to return to this injurious lifestyle is what warranted my fall.   Different sorts of dramatization with certain persons occurred, causing those that I associated with to react and respond in ways that I can not explain in detail!

In light of the decision I made pertaining to what I stated above, one day I was pulled over and taken to the police station where I was questioned, charged and taken to the county jail with a $150,000 cash bail.

From intake, I managed to call Aliah and received no answer. I was on 7-day lock-up in Camden County Jail. The 23« hour lock downs made it difficult to shower, use the phone and clean my room. So I would have to sacrifice a shower to get on the phone and vice versa. With continuous calling, I found out that S.D. was in Salem County Jail and had been since November 17, 1996. I was locked up on November 18th.

*****

April 1997, while awaiting trial, I was sent to Bordentown for a previous possession of a stolen handgun charge. I was given a 1 year sentence and served 9 months of that sentence before being sent back to the county jail to face my open charge.

The courts relaxed from the original plea deal of 25 years and came down to 20. After denying that agreement, they came down to a 15year plea with a 7 year stipulation.

I was classified to South Woods in order to fulfill my debt to society and finance a greater means than my incredulous mind could even comprehend at the time.

This of course was a reality far from the likes of an Ancient Athens punishment; well... the original likes of. Amerikkka has infringed upon numerous of cultures, policies and laws, making them their own with a few numbered twists in order to orchestrate the rise in Supremacy.

At 25 years old, I choicefully became a disappointment to my son, his mother and the rest of my family. Story of my life! (SMH!) Ordinarily, I would find some way to manipulate myself into undermining the actions I'd taken to reach the point of deserving the punishment given. Psychologically and realistically, what could've changed in my upbringing to prevent this mark of criminality and the stain that I put in my family legacy? So the punishment and debt was chiefly handed to my son's, their mother's and the rest of my family. For I had proven this true to be my society!

I started placing a number of requests in for vocational and educational classes. The means of purpose in me began to formulate! The expansion of my mental capacity began to take its

126

form! The once philosophical instructions that my family persisted to press upon me began to make all of the sense to me in the world! The numerous brothers who were being shipped from Trenton State Prison with 25 and 30 year sentences had become my mentors in law, history and just life in general.

I pressed on to champion in reconstructing the authentic me! It was now the year 2001, and subsequently to my change, I acquired my G.E.D! I was also awarded a certification in culinary arts, clothing industries (sewing, fabric cutting and mechanical skills), boot industrial shop and parenting life skills class. I was elated to present all of this good news to my family. They started to have hope and trust in me, and they actually believed this was the new me.

CHAPTER X
"MY GANS!"

Out of all the things in the world, history is the only thing that can record a man's life. I thought to myself, what is the point of living if no one remembers that you were here? If you do something, do the damn thing! Do it big or don't do it at all! When you check out, make sure they remember your name. Make sure enough was done, more good than bad!

*****

As time took its course, my grandmother's diabetes worsened, and she began to experience the effects of the disease. Her kidneys were failing, and she was in dire need of s kidney transplant. As many diabetics did, she had a catheter inserted in her arm and demanded weekly dialysis. My mother would keep me up to speed on my grandmother's health.

April 2001, I called home to inquire about my grandmother, because weeks prior the news got passed down that my mother was a match for my grandmother's kidney transplant surgery. I knew then that there really was a God! A mother and daughter kidney match; this was fit for a segment on the Oprah Winfrey show! Nevertheless, as our conversation progressed, things took an unexpected U-turn. My mother informed me that my grandmother had passed away! I was stricken with a sudden stimulant of panic. I had to fight to hold in the profanity that laced my mind, heart and soul! The conversation that I had with my mother, which was trustfully painful, was the most mind-opening exchanges that I ever took part in. My grandmother was never awarded the sumptuous opportunity to enjoy the real Daryl!

My mother ministered to me, speaking of good times, all my grandmother knew of me, seen in me and expected of me. After hanging up the phone, I retreated to my cell for a moment of peace and reflection. God did not make tear ducts for nothing, so I opened up the floodgates! I conflicted with tears of sadness and gratitude,

128

because I knew my grandmother had never forgotten my supreme place in life and home as a man of God, and no matter the presence of me being in the prison system, she still profoundly counted me as worthy and trusted me to ensure that the lineage is very much honored. Given the depth of this genuine truth, I succumbed to restoration.

*****

July of 2002, it was over a year that my grandmother had been laid to rest. My grandfather, the authentic patriarch that he was, continued holding the family up as best as he could. I would speak to him at least twice a week. I'll tell you, talking with my grandfather would cheer me up tremendously! I loved my grandparents past the identification of loves true meaning! They were such great human beings and raised 4 children in the shadows of themselves! Granted, everyone has their flaws. However, my aunts, uncles and of course my mother were pure in my heart! No matter what flaw...we always persevered as a family, no matter how improvident things may have looked or seemed!!!

CHAPTER XI

"A FEW SAD DAYS!"

There is a saying that has proven to be one of value: "Hang with those who have your answer and get away from those who have your problem!"

I ended up slipping back into my old ways! If a man cannot be humble it is likely that he cannot be still. And to be still is to be silent without motion. Every man should have or develop the ability to be still at some point, for it is the time where he can stop and hear his own thoughts--the time where he can consider or reconsider his past actions--the time he needs to think or better yet, pray!

The gang epidemic began to sweep the state of New Jersey and its prison system. Many of my associates fell into that sweep and the ones with rank started recruiting. At first sight, the movement looked real promising and galvanizing, witnessing such structured brotherhood, history, rules, regulations, oaths and pledges. The Bloods were a tough but strange; tenacious but different type of family. I began to give joining them some deep thought.

At this time, I was very well spoken, intelligent, pretty much well known and had secured plans, goals and endeavors. I ended up joining one of the factions of the Bloods street organization.

January 2005, I was paroled to a halfway back program. A halfway back is equivalent to a regular halfway house. My entire 8 years and 2 months in prison I wrote my son's and their mothers. I was also getting visits from multiple women and even dealing drugs towards the end of my bid to secure more money for my release. Truthfully, I'd missed the mark for maturation. My heart still just wasn't right. I was oh so close, but yet so far!

There was a home in the Fairview section of Camden secured by my sister, 'Ro'. Unbeknownst to me, upon being paroled there as planned, she had her boyfriend, his boy, her friend and her baby living there. This created a hazardous environment for me.

Aside from that, my family was elated to see me. Being the camouflaged individual that I was, I was able to play both sides. The Blood faction warranted my attention and expertise. This became a vacuum for all that I had planned and those who held high hopes for me.

Investing in the heroin trade, I began to take trips back to Newark, NJ to buy an immense amount of "bricks" (a brick is 50 $10 bags of heroin). My sister and her friend didn't work nor did they have motivation or ambition to get up and work. So, as a man, I always felt obligated to go get it for them.

By day I was attending the D.R.C (Day Reporting Center) for parolees on 17th street. I was sick of the stupid bus pass and depending on everybody other than myself. There's nothing wrong with buying a car, but the type of cars that I ended up buying were clearly out of the scope of normal. I will not go into details about these luxuries as it may seem as if I am glorifying my stupidity!

For the street culture, there are so many destructive elements which serve to annihilate ones abilities to maintain or retain his or her humanity and value. Amongst the youth are the older street heads who serve to extend psychological/educational trickery to the youth. They become void of compassion, bitter and even unconsciously murderous. I lived among these young men who offered nothing but helplessness and stifled premises of many under the banner of a gang culture. We had to be hard, because only us strong survive and "bang our colors" from a depth of common interest; and it is not a material factor... but an internal feeling of invisibilities, declining to recognize that we are the symbols of descending fallen creatures! I myself knew, not only what I had, but how much I had. On the real, I did not lose value, just the usefulness!

Many of my associates on 17th and Godfrey, in Philly became familiar with the gang life, but were not well versed. A few (not at all) began to evolve in this latest phenomenon and the life took off in the hood. On our block, this was bringing a lot of heat, hate and unwanted beefs. Due to the fact that I created a number of individuals under this Blood life, I was responsible for the supply and demand to combat the reality of the street wars that ensued. For the protection of people, places and things, I will not detail such graphics..... As dangerous and stressful--thank God--I'm still here with MY LIFE and not with "LIFE IN PRISON"!

A society's approach to punishment reveals its soul; how it understands cause and responsibility; what its utopian hopes are; and how it has decided to approach certain conflict.

While I had a decent, respectable job at the Camden aquarium, my activities in the streets formed an indirect window of suspicion in my parole officer to partially see. The acquisition of an abundance of materialistic and gang ties raised red flags (no pun intended). His suspicions warranted a phase of questions that began to annoy me, and reactionary measures prevented me from completing my parole period. The excessive arrogance, showing up to parole appointments late and very argumentized. I managed to last approximately 6 months in society! 6 MONTHS AFTER DOING 8« YEARS!!!

There are no life preservers nor life guards for this mishap of lame acts of regret in which I drowned in--trying to consume my last remainder of breath.

CHAPTER XII

"MY POP-POP!"

While back in prison, I was informed that my grandfather had contracted lymphoma cancer and he would begin his chemotherapy and radiation treatment. This news truly tormented me psychologically! 2 pillars from God that remained such a moral foundation for the family and now have succumbed to diseases that plagues humanity!

Then the news came that he had punched all on the cancer! It was in remission, and I was praying that it was not going to form against him again. But unfortunately, months prior to my release, he began to capitulate to the ills of the disease again. The once active, enthusiastic, passionate patriarch's condition had worsened, which led to many ailments he nor I had never foreseen. the more I thought of my grandfather's arduous position to fight, the more I wanted to fight for him! Isiah (54:4) says, "Surely he took up our pain and bore our suffering." I begged God to allow me to take my grandfather's pain.

April 17th, 2007, I was released and maxed out from Bayside State Prison. Christie was present to pick me up, and this was supposed to be again... a new lease on liberty!

Christie (Rest In Peace!) was actually a close relative of a member of Boyz II Men, and she was my girlfriend at the time. She was 5'5, about 140 lbs. and thick, brown eyes and brown skinned, very talented (song writer, singer, poet, and author), and personality wise, she was different! As I'm writing this book, I'm struggling to find words that are great enough to fit her personality. She was just that dope! She had 2 children, Chriss and Yazzy, whom I loved dearly and still do.

We immediately went to visit my grandfather, and I was told prior that he had lost weight. Although my incarceration served as a burden on the family due to my absence, my lasting hope was for him to forgive me for my many years of sinful actions! I really loved my grandfather for, he was my best buddy and mentor!

Finally arriving to the house, I was internally greeted with a flood of butterflies and happiness. This human emotion balanced and equal part of passion and dedication. My eyes felt like they had impatiently imparted from my eye-socket as I proceeded to see my grandfather.

The reality of us finally seeing each other and the unique solitaire embrace had brought God-filled tears of joy to the both of us. Though my grandfather had lost an enormous amount of weight and had other physical changes, I still saw him for all that I had ever known him to be, the large-spirited and powerful man that always labored tirelessly; a man who literally built his own house from the ground up for his wife and children; a man who was one of Conrail Train System's most influential workers; a man who sheltered, protected and breathed wisdom into me well into my twenties.

It was my grandfather's relationship examples with my grandmother that cultivated my identity on how to treat the person that I would someday give my life to. Although they wouldn't take root until later in my life, he planted seeds of responsibility in me.

We were able to unselfishly revisit many of the roots of historical value. You know... conversation that i wasn't articulate enough to have or mature enough to even understand.

My grandfather's wish was for me to selflessly give my life to God and be the man that my potential called me forth to be,. I see now that he was attempting to groom me to acquire the tools in order to build my own "Two Pillars"...

May 25, 2007... my grandfather completed his work and joined his beautiful wife with The Lord!

This day that I speak of was not an ordinary day at all! There was a host of family members that were there to celebrate all day and enjoy the company of each other. You know, family love. However, I was tremendously stricken with grief! It was deeper than I have ever grieved, because not only did I love my grandfather past the moon and back and valued his wisdom, but I never truly

134

experienced the pleasures of co-existing with him as a MAN! Going through the revolving door of the system prevented me from appreciating his presence. As I ponder on it now, I am just realizing the greatness in his presence that I so dearly miss every awakening day that I strive towards reaching the same levels of greatness that my grandfather had reached!

CHAPTER XIII

"PRECARIOUS PARADOX!"

"You can reach out only as far as you have traveled within. The journey is the same!"

-Unknown

My step-father graciously assisted in securing me a job in Temple University as a Computer Operator. I managed to live a productive comprehensible life. My grandfather would say, "Never let the sun beat you up!" So I was always out of the bed at approximately 5:30 in the morning, news on, fixing breakfast and making sure the kids got up for school. Christie worked the 7pm to 7am shift at Einstein Hospital.

Like any normal citizen, in the flow of the morning until my 2pm to 11pm shift began, I would run errands for her, shop, pay bills, etc. Sometimes she would be my accomplice in a trip to the gym if she wasn't tired from her shift. I would also drop the kids off at school and pick them up. Christie and I were a match made in heaven!

My job had reached a point where I was potentially ready for a jump into the union. I started to make all the imperative and strategic connections needed to secure my career; preparations for classes at Temple and career advancement. My family was honored and happy! Everything was taking its shape on its path of success according to everyone's prayers.

I was fortunate enough to acquire an additional family when the "Dark Syde" alliance movement took off. Music was a passion of mine, and I genuinely indulged in this productive communal venture, which comprised of 'Reality Childz', 'Sunny Drapes', 'Show', 'Bankz',

'Akbar', and family. The production of music, videos and shows in the city of Philadelphia; Dark Syde was another authentic provider of community fulfillment.

Every Father's Day, 13th and Courtland turned into a wonderland for kids, funded by the above-mentioned brothers; games, prizes, money, food, gifts and the availability of mentorship, you name it, it was in the cause! Reality Childz and family recognized the importance of it takes a village to raise a child, because he himself was raised by the village. We would work to keep them away from the strings that led down roads of failure. Mentoring to them became not just a job, but a natural part of our duties in the village being that we didn't want to see them going through the hardships that we had already endured.

Childz and I... though I could say that he is more than a Brother's Keeper--this conclusion would have to be biased with unfailing love and respect, considering the perspective of each personal character, naturally embraced and authenticity, along with my community of others that I mentioned prior. They strived to keep me sane.

Though I was this "So called" self-proclaimed family man, citizen, father, etc., by night I would change my entire persona, perpetuating my ignorance through gang activity. Despite the positive assignment I had with the authentic, loving family, music and Temple University family... I still unintellectually made it capable to fill my addiction in the streets. Sadly! But this is the substance of who I was at the time. It was easy to mask who I really was, because I was comfortable in my own skin of what I always persisted to do and to be.

As a black "Man", I've always directly dealt with the burden of ego, pride and identity. Much of my life I had denied truth despite it staring me directly in my face! The same truth that would have protected me from so much harm! Because of these rejected facts, I froze in seeking who I really was in such of an ill-equipped mind set. The depth of this criminal street addiction, I ignored! Nevertheless, I always returned to the substance masking my shame, to relax in comfort the torment of my intrinsic reality--that I was socially, emotionally and psychologically inadequate. Each denial amounted to nothing less than lies. Each lie serving a greater disease as blinders, hampering my potential to see the fact that destruction lie before me. Such a destruction that would culminate in my involvement in gang activity that would ultimately lead to the ultimate destruction of trust; trust of my son, family, Christie and her family, my music family, work family and even the families of the many people who were victims of my insidious criminal expose's.

March of 2008, uncredited with a geographical, racial world view and how it developed as a socio-cultural reality, which requires a whole new way of looking at human diversity in its many forms of Blackness around me; fortuitously, I prevaricated from such a love affair which should have become the firm brick and mortar in my steps back to King and Queendom. How blind was I?!? I mean... social Darwinism; yes, it's real and STILL RELEVANT! It was not only slavery that robbed Blacks here in Amerikkka of their identity. Far more powerful and telling has been not only the cruelty of racism, but *solipsism* and lack of communal education; the sumptuousness of material and financial focal points. We can only judge the future by what we've suffered from the past! The message is clear! To rely solely on ones own unimproved state of mind, my own limited thoughts without reading, learning and debating the thoughts of others, conversing meaningfully and studying from time to time, causes a man, woman or child to become small-minded, closed in and trapped inside this lonely, unconventional belief system of unworthiness that Amerikkka has attempted by many means to impart on and affect us subjectively.

Careful and voracious studying increases both the awareness, understanding and options! A man, woman or child without having knowledge of their lineage or historical values, is a hostage to their own faults!

Lulled by a cultural ethos promoting narcissism and pleasure, many Black men (like myself), women and youth have fashioned for themselves a new kind of identity in opposition as much as possible to that which I perceived as "white". "Blackness" has been defined

138

in many ways in terms of that which is banal and outrageous, but this was not seen by me nor my associates. I was saturated by hype and the glamorizing of what my optical system saw, in the streets, movies, sports and the media. Too many Blacks cling to a fabricated identity whose most oblivious characteristics are consumerism and status.

Those institutions that used to reflect the qualities of life in my grandparents and parent's marriages, that gave meaning to the Black communities have been eroded: the church, kinship, neighborhoods with caring elders, the preacher, the teacher, the barber, the store keeper, etc. Then the dignity and sense of achievement associated with work.

This banality and narcissism had sent me back to jail once again on March 27, 2008 for unlawful possession of a firearm, certain persons, unlawful possession of a handgun and attempted robbery. I was given a $150,000 cash bail.

I let down my family again! My son, Christie's son, daughter and family, my Temple University family, my music family and community of others, and my dear grandparents who were trusting in me from above!

I had lacked the necessary skills or proper education and spiritual enlightenment to enter and be successful in mainstream arenas. I NEEDED TO UNDERSTAND how to remove the barriers that kept me down...

I was bailed out on those charges pending trial or plea, whatever favored me. Gloria was now my other half. Considering the loss of Christie, I always had another woman to fall back on. I was suffering from the consequences of the oppressive and mean-spirited policies of my own lust. There's this cliché and ridiculous saying women use that says, "The best way to get over a man is to get under another one!" However, that just may be true for men as well, because for myself, when one female would not work out for me, there would be 3 or 4 in the shadows, waiting to take the other's place.

Like most women, the ones I dealt with were all convinced that I was different. It was either because they wanted to believe this or because I was able to convince them that I was different...

Karma is never too far away! In 2010, I was depleted of money. I knew that Gloria (an additional one of my kid's mother's) being pregnant and joyous as we were which ended up being a short-lived celebration, due in part to reality of lawyer money, bills and having kids to look after was quite relevant. I wanted to do the right thing by Gloria and my unborn son, just as I had planned to do with my previous kid's mothers, however, I still had this sick belief system in acquiring finances by way of the streets. If a hammer is the only tool in your tool belt, everything around you looks like a nail!

Before I made bail for the pending charges, while in the county, I still managed to stay in tune with the streets and those in them. Playing both sides, I'll admit, was ridiculously difficult!

Added were a few more pieces to my puzzle in an asset to what I tried to uphold and build on. My gang-related son (the apple doesn't fall too far from the tree), I called him 'Lil P', he was very sharp to be his age, in the streets and books. Despite the negative criminal belief systems, I would forfeit what we were into to focus more on what us Blacks needed to do that was positive, why we were doing what we were doing and what to do to fix it. These young or older guys, majority never even had a voice or in fact a REAL Black positive, trusting human in their lives. And I was able to provide wisdom, strength and commonality to their lives. Nevertheless, it was through the necessity of the streets. And one of the bonds were that, we "all" at some point experienced invisibility!

many of these minority youths today, not only are suffering the consequences of the oppressive mean-spirited policies of White Amerikkka, but they are descendants of men and women whose spirits were broken by these practices and who too often turned their pain and frustrations inward, then the floodgates open and you have gangs, murder, robbery, violence and broken families and communities.

The opportunity to provide my affiliates with greater means to reach a higher goal financially, as well as myself, felt like what I was supposed to be doing. An immense quantity of heroin was being sold and those who involved in its distribution evolved.

Under the pressure of what lie before me, I began to stress a lot with symptoms of paranoia and anger considering all of the drama that started to form around me. It felt like a symptom of claustrophobia, but in all reality, this was my conscious convicting me of my wrong-doings considering the Higher Power having a better plan for me to be More Than Just A Number!

Our bills were due, and I needed at least $50,000 saved. I also needed an additional $50,000 saved up for Gloria and the boys before or if I went to prison.

An unforeseen cost that I never pondered prior to making a decision that cost me my freedom and related to those "so-called" homies in our Blood gang faction. Of course most were not friends by far, but not surprisingly, the few that claimed to have respect and affection for me, while I thought to have been treating them accordingly, they slammed the door on my face. An affiliate of mine had continued with issues of coming up short with his end of the money that was supposed to be being earned with excuses that his drugs turned up missing, etc.

I sent a text to Lil P, and a text came back in return stating that he was with this said person and a homegirl. I learned that the best players in the game are the ones who learn the rules, master and manipulate them and come up with a few rules of their own. I thought it was as followed.

I sent a text back ordering Lil P to call a meeting. We would always meet in Marshall Estate Park, in the West Oak Lane section of Philly.

This night no one was to supposed to get hurt (I guess). It was a regular session, drinking, smoking and you know... discussing business. However, the more you drink and smoke, the more whatever the issues are that are on your mind begin to surface and things get violent. The issue of the drugs and money came up. Lil P grilled ole boy with questions, only after riding around with him all day, shopping, eating, messing with girls and buttering him up. As I chimed in to question him, he continued in his lies, but it was apparent to me and everyone else who was present that he was lying.

Lil P had become infuriated by this and looked at me... Then he popped (started beating dude up)! The other homies and I watched and laughed despite my anger towards dudes. As crazy as this may sound, this was at times normal in our gang culture. Majority of us got busy like this on the regular and would go right on about our business like nothing ever happened.

While we watched, I secretly instigated it on, fueling Lil P even more. I thought that we would all continue in our travels the next day. However, I would concede that this situation was different because of the amount of money that was involved. Truthfully...I even imagined someone would die that night. But contrary to what I was thinking, reality quickly smacked me that bills needed to be paid, money needed to be put up in the savings, etc. I should have known from the look on ole boy's face that he was nervous and worried.

The next day, I called 4 homies. We met up in the back of the Spanish store on 17th and Godfrey. We spoke about this dudes brother working for a certain corporation that had a chain of stores, and dude knew what store pulled in the greater amount of money. Prior to this, he was known to give us locations in the past that resulted in us coming up on nothing less than $27,000. True Story! I would break him off 5% off every joux. The last one, he admitted that he was done.

Lil P and I drove to Camden's Pine Point Park to meet dude. He was hesitant to convince his brother to do what needed to be done. He even called his brother on the phone, and his brother continued to refuse. So Lil P ended up throwing ole boy in the trunk and drove back to Philly swerving and doing hard turns to shake him up.

When he was let out of the trunk, he promised to convince his brother to set things up. The brother was sort of tough too! He didn't mind a little drama, but this was above his pay scale! Under threat and after being shot at by the homies, he promised to set it up.

When we dispersed from the park, my mind was everywhere. As acerbic as I seemed to be that night, doing the right thing was the furthest from my reasoning. In my purview was the fact that I had a family to take care of, and my money would be the foundation of their comfort. Not the legal way, or the patient way, but the "gangster" way, interrupting a life or lives to be exact.

"KEEPING IT REAL!"... to me, is a fear, however, that rests in this reality and beauty of what is accessible to me--that I will never be forever lost in the memories which have sustained my identity throughout the years of it. Keeping it real will never leave me trapped in anyone's social confinement of societies own making, where I may end up being a stranger if I don't answer this call of "gangster"!

My little homie insisted to go in place of me. For he felt he owed me something. I initially called this off! My conscious corrected me over and over. I lived in a cross-world, where my mental and emotional positives and negatives were cultivated through suffering and life's many tribulations. This world was fear...this place of human depravity and anguish. Yet...I earned it!

The weekend of the Mayweather and Sugar Shane fight my cousin threw a fight/birthday party. So I spent the weekend with my family. I was good in attempting to hide my business. On and off the phone, texting, I was setting things up. Monday was the day that the joux was to take place.

I drove in high speed back to North Jersey to pick up Gloria from work. I dropped her off then went back to Philly. Everyone met up at the studio/house at 5th and Grange to discuss a few things.

To kill some time, I went in the other room to play XBOX and think. I would always laughingly think of conversations my mother

143

and I would have. I'd think of her saying, "If it wasn't for bad luck, I wouldn't have none..." among other things. My mother's my best friend and knows me better than anyone besides God and my stepfather. We really had a wonderful relationship, and I was thankful for it. This has had turned around in my psyche while playing... my son's, my life and my future.

May 5, 2010...It was still time to repent from not only the action that was to take place, but the initial belief and world system that has plagued the children of the most high since the corrupted seed: God had appointed Adam dominion and leader, and due in part to Adam's disobedience in Genesis chapter 3, God cursed man and woman for their disobedience. God had just spelled out what would happen, because Satan was able to enter God's world and inject his malicious intent. Unbeknownst to me, this infection desired to run its course.

Time to keep it real... My homie called the person to double check our plans and make sure everything was still the same, and it was confirmed by both him and his brother that everything was good. I had always prided myself in being a strategic planner when it involved anything that was imperative to one's life, saving it and preserving it. So I would reconstruct someone else's plan to fit how I seen fit when it involved street business.

My associates and I arrived in the area. I still had a chance to turn away from this activity, but at this point, the right thing to do was the furthest from my mind, heart and soul. The right thing to me at the moment was to go get this money!

In going forward, we rushed in with demands. 4 people cooperated quickly. However, there were 2 additional individuals, which was more than what was explained to us. It was too late to turn back though! I was already engaged! In my mind was that tormented pain-that inability to let go of the agony of the streets! My life... prison, those around me, ignorance, verbal abuse, failure, misdirection and conspiring.

I was parlous to these people; emotionally, physically and even to their families and mine. The safe was our focal point, which ended up not being what we were told would be there.

Managing to escape undetected, approximately a quarter mile away I noticed us being followed onto the highway. At this time a chase ensued with numerous police cars trailing us. I was furious and determined to elude the law.

This was not how this joux was supposed to go. How did we get on someone's radar to even be followed? By happenstance, we briefly avoided the law, giving us enough time to get out of the car and split up. I sent him back to Philly with the money. I disappeared into a friend's house in Paulsboro. So concerned with eluding the detection of the law, it fell upon me that I had lost my phone. I immediately retreated in panic. I was hoping I didn't leave it in the car!

An hour later, I received a phone call from Gloria with the aggravating news that the detectives had notified her and invaded our residence, disturbing the stillness and peace of my home as she was awakened from her and my unborn child's rest. What was I to do now? How'd they even end up at my house? Damn!!! This was The Cost of "Keeping It Real"!

When I would get into trouble, the very first thought that would cross my mind (besides trying to get away) was my parents and family. My greatest memories center around my mother, father, grandparents and family and how important they are to me... how they managed to fuse their teachings upon a hard, knuckleheaded and disobedient Daryl. I seemed to never really care about nothing but ME!

I refused to go on the run, because I knew how disrespectful robbery/homicide could be, running up in family's houses, unexpectedly disturbing their peace. I had done enough. So I arranged to turn myself in with the assistance of an attorney.

Entering the police station, I knew this would probably be my last taste of freedom. I had refused to answer any questions in their interrogation. They asked about the money and the second party, and my actual response was, "Me no speaka no engli!"

The detective vowed to not only charge me with everything he could, but publicly humiliate me as well and send me to the county jail.

Meanwhile, my conscience zeroed in on my family, my son's, Gloria and even the victims in that establishment that was victimized. Was I now regretting that I was "Keeping It Real"? because while I was keeping it real, I had just caused an enormous amount of people I loved great pain, great worry and great suffering! While I was keeping it real, I embarrassed my family, and more so my sons, putting them through more hell than they had already been through at my hands. Every Homie isn't your homie, because while Keeping It Real, one of them set me up and had them waiting for us!

My bail totaled almost a million dollars! I was sick! My mother, father, sons, sisters, brothers, Gloria, work, walks, the pool, driving, eating good, watching movies, Reality Childz, Sunny Drapes, Akbar, Show, Bankz, my cousins, aunts, uncles, etc; all of these wonderful beings and things would turn into collected memories during the walk of shame through this upcoming bid...

All of them respectfully held their special objectivity and spiritual design in cultivating the personality that stood within me. Sad that I was left with these tragic reminders of what was and (or) what could've been.

In that cell--cold and alone--I had greatly been humbly reduced to this ground of paralysis emotionally, mentally and physically unable to operate more to express my humanity. I had spent a large part of my life in and out of prison...I was sick and tired of being sick and tired of what I was going through....in and out of the streets and my family's lives; living the dreadful existence of society's banished, back to prison.

Although these memories are true, they really are a reduction of lies from such a painful reminder of a past that have pierced my life, my soul, which now has caused bouts of depression. Who am I even?!? What am I?!? Where am I?!? When will I?!? Again...my fondest memories are a nucleus around my grandparents, my mother, father, son, sisters and family! It is very painful to even reflect on how wonderful this community of love who gave all they had to me; in fact, when, considering a great deal of my life, I gave in return... I gave little to nothing!

Early in my incarceration, in the county jail, I was forced to reflect upon my fatherhood. I love my sons more than anything in the world! My best friends in heart, mind and soul! I left them all alone in a such a world that cares less for minorities who are subject to attack on their Blackness, and creating a vacuum in a culture that already has plagues of disunity. They have to fend for themselves without the protection of their father and mentor. Therefore, my existence in my boys lives in all reality was a non-existent reality, in light because I was still Just A Number. I wasn't a cognizant, real Black father! I mean... not because I didn't love but because I didn't understand the magnitude of paternal love. Yes... I seen it daily, my grandparents, father and mother, my uncle Kevin and Patti Ann, etc... I was busy "Keeping It Real"! I felt no true obligation to a God Given blessing called "fatherhood" that was given. My potential, priorities and love were clearly misplaced and of course negatively manufactured by my choices of living the street life--partying, chasing money, sexual promiscuity and manipulation...

I would also often think in depth about what would have taken shape if I'd managed "the man" in myself as my step-father, grandfather, great grandfather and uncles had; that counselor, provider, protector and advisor for family and community. If I were always willing to sacrifice anything but my relationship with God for the sake of my children! Never from the care of a jail/prison slave camp, but from the blessing of our home, married, being a positive example and raising them to be Real Men!

147

Just think... If I was there to nurture, assist in their cultivation and be that energetic, cool, hip, intelligent father my kids knew me to be...

As a result of my ignorance, from a dark place of selfishness in my life, my kids seat that was specially reserved for their lives continued to come up empty... Where is dad?

I blame only my insidiousness and my choices for leading me to my confinement and leading my sons to emotional confinement as well! (SMH!)

My actions from "Keeping It Real" caused my victims and their families a great deal of pain and suffering as well! Over the years, I have been incapable of answering the call of apology. Through my monumental window of disappointment, while sittin in my cell aware of my loved one's disappointments, I began to have continuous epiphanies. I was able to see the magnitude of hurt that I brought upon my famili, my victims and my victims' families, because the people who love and care for these victims are hurt as equally and painfully!

During my street days, I was lost in this need to route my way through life accumulating A NUMBER of things that brought hurt to so many people! Admittingly, I was so lost in a need to be accepted and to feel as though I was somebody. I now had to detox from this "street life", because it was a drug that diseased my body, and I started to have withdraw from trying to stray away from it.

The courts were offering me 25 years for my part in the joux and 15 if I would tell them who my accomplice was. However, I chose to protect the other guilty party as well as my street credibility amongst the number of my affiliates in Philly.

Meanwhile, I was preparing for trial on the 2008 charges that were still pending. My attorney, who was a sharp brother from Newark, NJ, was a fighter, but I took a victim stance, stressed, scared and angry. Finding out "The Homie" was prepared to testify against me infused my emotions even more. I blamed my lawyer, claiming that he wasn't fighting hard enough. I blamed the judge; I even verbally assaulted him numerous times for not seeing the loopholes in my case. I came to blame my homies for not finding the 2 brothers that were telling and taking care of them. You know... "deading" the threat of a possible testimony. I even had the audacious nerve to blame my parents for lack of things and even living on a drug block. In ignorant fashion, I went so far as to blame the school system for their lack of enthusiasm in teaching, etc...

I started to think that damn near everyone was against me! Man... I blamed everybody and everything except for the real person who was truly to blame: ME! Still, I wanted to change! If not... God, then please just take me home! If I can't help than God surely don't allow me to hurt anyone anymore!!!

I started attending church, bible study and even those NA (Narcotics Anonymous) meetings. I was seriously weather-beaten and empty, in need of fulfillment and light in this relentless darkness. However, prison is such a miserable place, where ignorance and anger are welcomed and embraced by the administration and staff, because without it they wouldn't have jobs. Those who strive to rehabilitate themselves or usually effected by angry or racist officers and (or) angry and frustrated prisoners. To my point, the one working so hard to change can become frustrated themselves. Let's say you're housed in a place like South Woods Prison, where there is every vocational trade available that you could think of and the ability to get certifications in these trades; the thoughts of finding employment haunts a man that has kids and a wife...The first plague that effects the mind of a Black Brother is that criminal record! W.E.B DuBois said: "The first thing and almost universal device was to use the courts as a means of re-enslaving the Blacks, It was not then a question of crime but rather one of color that settled a man's conviction on almost any charge." Amerikkka uses this tool to burden our psyche into believing this system to the point of our demise! Though the above statement of W.E.B BuBois is true, however, the standard of a house lies in the legs of the MAN!

It's true that social inequality lies to be a burden in the Black and Hispanic community; high unemployment and the lack of industries to fit our population in urban areas. Therefore, we must hold these state and local representatives highly accountable and responsible. I mean, while a Brother or Sister strives to rehabilitate there is still this haunting thought of the Government policies that choke the necks of the average working-class minority. These instrumental and intrinsic goods that industries base their corporations (government entities) on, act in the best interest of "their own" (the privileged), but that doesn't fix unemployment for "us" (the underprivileged)!!! For example: when the manufacturing of clothing in the U.S. moved to China, it resulted in astronomical numbers of unemployment in minorities causing us to fall below the poverty line.

The absence of socialism reports poor fiscal and monetary policies that weigh heavily on communities, which by far makes it all the more difficult for a man or woman to transition back into society with even the skills they acquire while incarcerated. This perhaps can induce a form of melancholy.

Oh yes... Then, what about the individuals that suffer from emotional and social inadequacies, that have been gang-banging for a great deal of their lives and have become so cynical and untrusting of people that all they know and feel comfortable with is gang members? They don't feel welcomed by mainstream society. The belief system of a life-long gang-banger is a strong and tough system to break, especially when you've been betrayed, let down, hurt, and talked down to by not only white sub-superiors, but Blacks as well. You try so hard to place your best foot forward to the beat of your tiredness, but the other foot is dragged by the other part of your brain that is addicted to a counterproductive belief system. In these cases, church, bible study and education become null and void!

"THE BIGGER PICTURE!"

Prison isn't much different than the streets. Therefore, it was still easy for me to perpetuate my ignorance while having a desire to want change. Gang-banging, drug-dealing, gambling... You name it, I was in it. I was in Bayside Prison and in the loop. I was doing whatever it took to keep me from dealing with my internal demons and facing my fears. I fought, because as humans we are transferring agents of our feelings and emotions. If I was hurt, you'll hurt with me! It was easy for me to transfer my feelings and emotions physically, because I was talented with my hands.

*****

In 2012, I signed my trial papers for August 6, 2012. If I were to lose, I would be given 168 years to life in prison. However, my attorney negotiated from 25 years, to 20 years, and was now at a 15 year plea agreement. I was confident in going to trial! My mother attempted to convince me to take the plea. She said, "Fifteen you have a chance of coming home, but one hundred sixty-eight years to life?" I was certain of my attorney and his representation though.

During visits from Gloria, we would enjoy and appreciate the time given. For me, the visits were also bittersweet, because she and the kids didn't deserve to be subjected to the procedures that came with visiting a loved one in prison. Officers are disrespectful and ignorant, treating the visitors as if they're confined as well. Though we both loved each other and looked forward to visits, they tormented the both of us!

I remember when my son XyQuan was born November 11, 2010...I cried! I didn't just cry in joy, but in sorrow! I'm not this man that doesn't take care of his responsibilities, but that's what I was reduced to. Here I was 2 years after my son was born in a slave camp with Gloria raising my son without me!

As time passed, the change in her began to be noticeable. She wasn't too joyful when we spoke on the phone or even in visit, and she appeared weary. When asking if she was okay, she would always assure that she was good. However, wisdom is like deep water... You only see or know the surface, but never the bottom line. She was suffering from loneliness and frustration. Like most women, she needed the comfort of a man, comfort that I wasn't able to give her. Though I tried to assure her that everything would be okay with letters, cards, and all the wisdom I had, deep down inside we both had little to no more confidence in what was really left.

The visits ceased to exist. Then the calls stopped. The mail and money orders halted. At such a traumatic and critical time of my life, I stood alone to fight the masses in the courtroom! How could this be? I lost my lady and my youngest son; in turn losing a big part of myself! Though I couldn't blame him, my oldest son was estranged! I abandoned him at the most imperative times for a father to be in a son's life. So what did I really expect? My decisions brought about ravaging effects to my family and Gloria. Then, when your emotions begin to consist of these disruptive changes, it's either fight or flight! However, it seemed as though I forgot a main ingredient to fixing a problem, which is finding a solution. Lack of communication with my kids had really taken a toll on my heart, and in spite, I punished others out of my frustration and ignorance.

Then, you instantly grow weary, tired, feeble and sick of this unforeseen Cost that I never pondered before making the decisions that caused me to spend a great deal of my life in prison. I was starting to see that some of my "friends" were never really friends at all. In my absence, very few people have honestly and faithfully answered the call of REAL friendship and (or) companionship. I started wonder if ANYBODY that I ever called a friend was worthy of that title!

Truthfully, a significant answer hollered the discovery after a passage of time. My having to suffer adversity alone, aside with a fruit of abandonment displayed and fortified my conclusion that 90% were never really "Keeping It Real" or were true friends! I mean, I wasn't necessarily expecting people to financially provide for me, but send a card, pictures, a letter... I'm More Than Just A

Number! I'm more than a statistic! Don't count me out, then count me in when it is convenient to you. However, the world is full of these people.

I began to pray hard! My first time actually on my knees was June 3, 2013. Returning from a court trip, I was grateful to have received a 10-year sentence that I had to do 85% of. Instead of praising my lawyer, I praised God! In my cell, I prayed for almost an hour and a half, and through the grace and mercy of God, I began to see the light of God! I mean...I was literally internally broken, which I gave up as my offering! In the song "Take Me To The King" by: Tamella Mann, she said: "Take me to the King... I don't have much to bring.../ My   heart is torn to pieces... That's my offering..."

That was exactly how I felt. I was finally submitting to the King!

My parents were getting older, family members were getting sickly and passing away, and my sons needed their father. My absence had even taken a toll on a young proxy that I had mentored and practically raised back in Philly. He backslid and ended up "allegedly" committing a gang-related homicide. This young man that I'm speaking of was 26 years of age when I was home. He didn't like nor trust me when we first got introduced. Like any other young brother from an urban area, he had seen and experienced the ruins of morals, principles and values from the ones that claimed to love and care for him. With our young brothers, parents let them down, old heads use them and throw them away, etc... But me, I was authentic with him. There were never any strings attached! When I heard about what happened with one that I considered a protege of mine, I knew I
HAD TO CHANGE!

So I let go and let God! He began to work His magic in me! I had to leave the gang-banging alone. You know...stay out of the descriptive chaos, which is not easy might I say, especially in prison. What do I tell my homies back in Philly? They'll lose respect for me! Will I be able to go back as a new man without criticism?!? Because in this life, this twisted culture, young brothers don't take this sort of thing lightly and will literally try to blow your head off for even attempting to abandon your rank!

The most arduous task of my life began! I still experienced the residuals of my old ways, because when you begin to change in prison, people don't always take kind to the sort of transformation that doesn't condemn their misery and neediness. They take it as a sign of weakness, like a man who gives his life to God isn't built Ford tough or something! Or they assume that you think you're better than them. Then your "so-called" friends and homies want to call in for favors, the kind of favors that bring trouble. Still, at times you may feel obligated to assist, and in prison...

As an example, I will mention a specific incident that occurred when I was in Bayside Prison. Someone took it upon themselves to steal from one of my homie's room. This person thought that I would turn the other cheek and talk it out, but stealing from a person's cell was a no-no!!! And stealing from a gang member stamped a person's death certificate. I was feeling like the entire prison would judge me if I didn't handle the situation. I was worried about what "my hood" (my specific Blood set) would think... If I did nothing, then this would invite more individuals to do the same to me or anyone in my hood. There was no telling. Being labeled a rat can get you hurt or even murdered in prison. So I decided to confront the dude who was of another hood. We ended up fighting in the room, and if other members of my hood didn't intervene, then the outcome would've been critical, murderously! Blood (literally) was everywhere in the room, and the police didn't care. Bayside is such a racist prison that they loved when we fought and tried to kill each other. In their heads, they were probably saying, "Look at those niggers killing each other!" Listen to this:

"...KKK CONGRATULATES GANG-BANGERS FOR SLAUGHTER OF BLACK PEOPLE

(Following is a letter which is being circulated around the Milwaukee area and other cities where there is a high crime rate among Blacks.

154

The courier finds itself in the position to let people know what is being said regarding this issue.)

THE KLU KLUX KLAN WOULD LIKE TO TAKE THIS TIME TO SALUTE AND CONGRATULATE ALL GANG-BANGERS FOR THE SLAUGHTER OF OVER 4,000 BLACK PEOPLE SINCE 1975. YOU ARE DOING A MARVELOUS JOB. KEEP KILLING EACH OTHER FOR NOTHING. THE STREETS ARE STILL NOT YOU NIGGERS... IT IS OURS. YOU ARE KILLING EACH OTHER FOR OUR PROPERTY. YOU ARE KILLING WHAT COULD BE FUTURE BLACK DOCTORS, LAWYERS AND BUSINESS MEN THAT WE WON'T HAVE TO COMPETE WITH. AND THE GOOD THING ABOUT IT IS THAT YOU ARE KILLING THE YOUTH. SO WE WON'T

HAVE TO WORRY ABOUT YOU NIGGERS IN GENERATIONS TO COME. WE WOULD FURTHER LIKE TO THANK ALL OF THE JUDGES WHO HAVE SENTENCED THOSE NIGGERS TO PRISON.

WE ARE WINNING AGAIN. PRETTY SOON WE WILL BE ABLE TO GO BACK TO RAPING YOUR WOMEN, BECAUSE ALL OF THE MEN WILL BE GONE.

SO YOU GANG-BANGERS... KEEP UP THE GOOD WORK. WE LOVE TO READ ABOUT DRIVE-BY SHOOTINGS. WE LOVE TO HEAR HOW MANY NIGGERS GET KILLED OVER THE WEEKENDS. WE CAN TOLERATE THE NIGGERS WITH JUNGLE FEVER (FOR NOW)... BECAUSE THAT FURTHER BREAKS DOWN THE RACE. TO ALL GANG-BANGERS ACROSS THE WORLD; WE DON'T LOVE YOU NIGGERS, BUT WE CAN APPRECIATE YOU GANGBANGERS. YOU ARE DOING A WONDERFUL JOB IN ELIMINATING THE BLACK RACE. WITHOUT THE MEN... YOUR WOMEN CANNOT REPRODUCE... UNLESS OF COURSE, WE DO IT FOR THEM. THEN WE WILL HAVE SUCCESSFULLY ELIMINATED A RACE THANKS TO YOUR HELP AND COMMITTMENT TO KILLING EACH

OTHER. IF MOST OF YOU NIGGER GANG-BANGERS CANNOT
READ THIS LETTER, IT IS OKAY. GO PULL A TRIGGER
AND KILL A NIGGER..."

Wow!!! Do you see the textual evidence that has been placed before you that is still relevant as I pen this truth between these lines? For example: look at Donald Trump and his constituents (Roy Moore) wanting to abolish all amendments after the 10th. If you're familiar with the amendments, then you would see that what they're basically is that they want to legally re-institute slavery.

CHAPTER XV

"REVELATION: REDEMPTION; GREAT I AM!"

I started to pray and meditate on my actions as I sat alone in the room after washing the blood off my hands. It was apparent that I was good with my hands, but at what Cost? For, what do I even have to prove anymore to the unproductive people who could care less about me and my family? When you do things to hurt yourself, you hurt those that love you as well!

I began to understand that this a test from God! It made me realize that I still had an enormous amount of growing to do. I could say with conviction that I was a MAN yet. I was still becoming that MAN! I had grown up psychologically, chronologically and even religiously and intellectually, but emotionally I remained an adolescent.

Remember, image is everything to this new ideological culture of masculinity among the youth and men. However, the day after that incident in Bayside, I made a vow to myself and a promise to God that I would never again make a decision based on how someone else viewed me! I put my pride to the side and stopped allowing others to control my life, because this is what image does when it is misconstrued into street mediocrity and white Amerikkka's psychological injection. I soon realized that the same kind of thinking that drove me to worry about being accepted by others was the same kind of thinking that led me to the streets in the first place. Now here I was sitting in prison suffering from this identity crisis1 Either I was God's son, or the street/the devil's son!

I no longer approved of this man, father, brother, son, nephew, cousin, uncle and friend that I was trying to be! I was working towards finding who I really was...

*****

The tutelage of my parent, grandparents and other positive and wise men and women began to spring from my subconscious.

Quotes such as, "The longest journey you'll ever take is the trip from your head to your heart," started making sense to me. I was also taking in wisdom from other prisoners, social workers, officers, and even old comrades. Yes... old homies! They spotted my potential. I was even fortuitous enough to have met a beautiful woman while I was in Bayside that, who along with others, claimed to have interest in the God in me! It is best to leave out the details of how we met, but it was similar to the Ruth and Boaz story in the Bible. She graciously made mention of the abilities in me. She was a Godfearing woman, from what I discerned. She knew the Bible very well, had a wonderful personality and she was a great mother!

The real people in my life weren't passing judgment on my present and past flaws, but they were seeing the greatness in me. They persisted to introduce me to a different world to help build with God, the village and historic nature that were awaiting within.

Prior to meeting God and persisting a relationship with Him, I knew little about the greatness of Him. But I couldn't sit still long enough to get to know Him, myself, nor anyone that was good for the greater part of my life. Psalms 46:10 say, "Be still and know that I am God!" This isn't just a physical demand; this is a spiritual demand within itself!

I began to study and open up my mind to the likes of Biblical theology, philosophy, science and psychology. Instead of wasting money on commissary, I would invest in books. And the Bible became my best friend. Reading as well as studying became second nature for me. In the meantime, I did not only have a plan to reconstruct myself for myself, but this was also for God, my son's, my parents, etc. I also began to formulate business plans.

I was eventually transferred Northern State, and if you are not familiar with the name, it is like the Mecca of all gangs! It is a prison that breeds destructive elements of danger, where prisoners either are gang members or basically castaways, in a system that is ran by a board of corrupt masters! The Department of Corrections is nothing but a big political maze that has the potential (if you allow it to) to stunt your growth and stagnate your development. However, like that saying, "Only the strong survive!" Myself and my community of others were blessed enough to be David's in this world of Goliath's (If you're not familiar with the story of David and Goliath, then open up your Bible to: 1 Samuel chapter 17).

Unfortunately, there are prisoners that are not free enough in spirit to share the same spiritual strengths that I was blessed with. However, I pray that they become aware of the power of God in them, because at times within their journey of doing time, prisoners become dangerously numb, lacking   their necessary emotional intellect, which causes them to disconnect from their natural humanity and the ability to righteously change.

How would I handle this atmosphere? Oh, I realized that God was sending me another test!!! Where will I rank in the pantheon of God's elect to keep this spiritual walk?!? Still, I focused on my plans, my goals and endeavors. In my favor, I was introduced to brothers with the same exact directions as I, men that challenged my thinking, my belief systems, as well as my vernacular.

"The secret of change is to focus all of your energy, not on fighting the old, but on building the new!"

-Socrates

My brother in Christ, Darryl (ironic, right?) introduced me to the likes of Fredrick Nietzsche, Michael Jung, Diop, and John Bonaparte, etc. We would elaborate on subjects from the Bible, history, current events, even diatribe about politics. The brother had 27 years in prison, so he would always say, "Never look back, the future awaits a great man's journey!" which calls to mind Philippians (3:13-14). So I pressed on towards the mark and forgot about what was behind.

I became a voracious reader and a study fanatic. My way of thinking had also become an evolution of time, strengthening my

159

perception as well as my purview of life which stretched beyond my circumstances.

Then the opportunity to take college courses became available by the request of a close friend I came to know whose interest in me was evident. Despite her professional and ethical position, she championed in assisting me, which was a beautiful thing.

While I awaited entry into the NJSTEP (New Jersey Scholarship Transformative Education in Prison) program, the brother 'Sal', who also had over 20 years in prison, invited me to partake in their mentor program, which is called "I.E.B.C" (Inmates/individuals Embracing Better Choices). I was sort of hesitant to jump into this group, because I had preconceived notions that it would be like all of the other programs that the prison system offers, ineffective! But this program was not one constructed by the Department of Corrections. It was "For Us, By Us!" All participants were real and genuine. We discussed real issues that plagued us as minorities. We even built on politics and law at times. So I became a mentor for the young brothers and I was mentored as well.

I joined the prison ministry with excitement, Bible study and even the choir. I faithfully participated in the latter half of what I had been grilled with all my life, and I started finding out that there was wisdom that lie dormant in me!

It is said that, power is primarily a make-up of factors such as a sort of spiritual vitality, emotional and physical strength, skills, time, education and social supports. As you see, I failed to mention finances, right? Because money is a powerful substance no doubt, but it is one that majority of the Amerikkkan people damage themselves and sell their souls for.

The devil continued to lurk in the shadows and threw temptations at me in an attempt to get me back in his car. But Matthew (4:4-11) became such a powerful vehicle to rest in...(LOL!)...Drive God!

The transformation of my mind, heart and soul pushed me into the necessary circles, which afforded me the ability to evolve even more. I was a little reluctant to attend these college courses, because all this productivity was still new to me. In my mind, there were still voices of self-doubt (the devil), telling me that I wasn't smart or ambitious enough; that I still loved the streets! So I prayed hard man!!! I immersed myself into the Bible and worked towards arming myself every day, from sun up to sun down. First thing in the morning, I was up thanking God for allowing me to see the light of another day. The that mystical voice of reasoning began to take over in me, and I felt the presence of God's 10,000 angels covering me.

My actions were in rhythmic cadence with my thoughts and words. There was a voice telling me that I was a King and one of God's chosen men/disciples. My mother had pressed on towards the mark out of her struggles and acquired college degrees! My step-father had been an accomplished Black man, regardless of his trials and tribulations! My sister, Nae, through the loads of mountains she faced, she still championed over them! My son DayQuan (such a strong young man he is!) had been emotionally resilient, even though not having his father around, pressed on to earn a college degree (which made me extremely proud to be his father). This was my chance to rise above and beyond and make my family proud to call me their, father, son, brother, cousin and uncle...

I ended up answering the availability and took full advantage of the college program without informing my family in the beginning. I had done enough talking in the past. So I was through speaking about change. I was more or less prepared to just change and allow my actions to speak for me!

I wrestled with my motives, wondering to myself if I was doing this to impress people in hindsight of the guilt I held so deeply within. The more I became conscious, the more guilt rung my heart, mind and soul. I mean, the guilt was really weighing heavy on me. This was a struggle for me to overcome!

My companion, Maranetta (who I mentioned earlier) and I remained committed to spiritual growth. My step-sons, Rashad, Rico and Rafiq started taking that trip from Philly to Newark, NJ to come and visit me. Now, with DayQuan, Xyquan, Rashad, Rico,

161

Rafiq, and Maranetta, (My Ruth) God gave me another blessing and purpose to press on with.

Suddenly, it wasn't just an opportunity to take a few college courses and impress people. This immense, infinitive realization of truth now illuminated everything in my journey. I had a perfect shot at educating myself, expanding my thinking and vocabulary and working on my presentation as a conscious Black man. I was ready to join the ranks of my step-father, grandfather and the rest of the patriarchs in my lineage. My companion even extended her interest in higher learning to join the historical likes of accomplished Black women such as, Mary France Berry, Marion Thompson Wright (who in 1940 became the first Black woman to earn a Ph.D in history and wrote the first mainstream academic book on the history of Black women), Mary Mcloud Bethune, Sue Bailey Thurman, Juanita Mitchell, Dorothy Porter and many others who were active in al sorts of Black historical preservation in the Jim Crow Segregation Era.

College became a tremendous challenge! I was not the sharpest butter knife in the drawer. I was a bit dull and rusty. However, tutors from Rutgers assisted me in improving on my math skills. Professors that I would be challenged by became my source of after class diatribes. Along with positivity comes negativity as well! Many interruptions arose that tried to prevent me from completing God's plans for me. (LOL!) They tried! But God walked with me as I continued to pursue my associated degree in Liberal Arts! Now I could proudly say I was a Norman/Spencer, and I no longer felt like such an embarrassment to my lineage. Now I was productively representing for the same family that I had caused so much pain and suffering to over the years, the ones that I kept up at night when I didn't come home, and I was out in the streets doing God knows what... my sons and their mothers who I left unattended to fend for themselves.

Being a graduate and who I am today is something I couldn't even imagine 7 years ago. That's ironic, right? 7 is God's number of completion in Genesis chapter 1.

There was no doubt in my mind that I wanted and needed to make good on this new beginning and be the man God created me to be; the man my grandfather, biological and step-father and uncles had become. I just didn't see it! And for the first time in my life I had a vision!!!

Many of my professors were from Rutgers, and I believe that the relationships I had with them is what laid out the educational foundation I so desperately needed in order to become a 3.6 GPA student. I now know my purpose in life! I wish to provide intellectual, political and historical acuteness to impoverished and struggling communities!

I was fully aware of the fact that my past would not be ignored or downplayed. It was once something that I was ashamed of. Nevertheless, my scars as well as my loved one's scars, are evidence and perfect wounds of survival. So I am not glorifying all of the wrong that I had done, but I am "REPPING MY SCARS!" (#REP YA' SCARS)...Jesus repped his scars. God's grace was strong enough to have washed the shame, guilt and sins off of me. Although I put my loved ones through so much, I was still blessed with the opportunity to educate myself and speak to the youth from an authentic heart, mind and soul, to turn ignorance and negligence into intelligence and nutrition...

In my abridged version of this book, I posed questions like, how could I ever fix the turbulent life I put my family through? And if I could exchange my life for the life of a perfect man, son, brother, father, etc... Was this all in God's plan and goal to promote my family and I? How do I make amends?

I accepted responsibility for my role in the destructive road that culminated in my past involvement with the street life, a Cost that weighed its worth in rocks. But with pressure and fire, my Higher Power polished me into a Ruby.

I am exponentially not the person that I was yesterday. For, I continue to evolve, adding more tools to my toolbox and building the necessary wisdom and strength that will house the beauty of humanity.

Now I was hopeful that through an audacious service provided through my life experiences, my philanthropic work would graciously allow me to partner with anyone, to reach out to our Black youth, men and women, and our communities. Then we could unify the hearts, minds and souls of our people, educate them and give them positive direction.

We are more than just a number here in the United States of Amerikkka. As I pen these words, the race ideology is already beginning to disintegrate as a result of 21st century behavior changes (race, identity, gender, history, ethnicity and culture). The consequences of this ideology is that, like gender and race, with its accompanying notions of color, men are not simply born, they are made.

Norma Fuller's choice of words implies that, "A man is not born a man"; that is a title earned through action, often violent action or currency, cars, clothes, women, houses, etc...

I made the conscious decision to not allow ANYTHING to dictate my future, but God! These said values that came from my parents, grandparents, the Bible and other books, school and some wise brothers transformed me and also so many other lives around me. Although majority of my life was spent behind blinders and bars, I am grateful to have met a great deal of "Real" positive brothers! There are some that will be released into society as prayerfully, changed, educated and productive men. However, there are the unfortunate whom will spend the rest of their natural lives in prison, or just about. I will continue to keep this torch lit for my brothers and sisters and fight against this systematic genocide; I will fight to bring change to social policies and socio-economic and community dysfunctions.

Mass incarceration remains a horrible epidemic here in Amerikkka, especially among minorities. The typical response from law makers is harsh criminal laws that do very little to solve the problems in our lives and our communities. It's a shame that there are more Blacks and Hispanics unemployed than there were slaves; the same slaves that were tricked, beaten, kidnapped and brought to the "U-lying States of Amerikkka!" (hashtag that)

We have to be vigilant and alert, because the devil roams about like a roaring lion, waiting to devour whom he can! These corporations (prisons) are bursting at the seams with unfortunate, impoverished and emotionally beaten young men. And sadly, there has even been an up rise in women being incarcerated at alarming NUMBERS! If we are not incarcerated, we are stuck on probation or parole, which is only a system to keep us in the system. And with the absence of the MAN from the home, our children suffer! I know mine have!!!

It is time to make real sacrifices to bring out solutions and change in the way we interact, think and respect one another. If these detrimental trends do not cease to exist, then an entire generation of young and older men, women and children will spend the rest of their lives either in dilapidated circumstances, in prison or dead!

True power is not found in the prancing around of a betrayer. We have work to do my Black and Hispanic brothers and sisters. true power is found soulfully in the intrinsic nature of our most primitive historical ancestral roots! we must strive to discover these roots day in and day out and educate ourselves to become MORE THAN JUST A NUMBER!

"So let go and make room for what's next. Let go and enjoy not knowing. Let go and be open to ALL possibilities, let go for greater peace of mind. Let go and see who is there!"

-Unknown

THE COST of any decision that we ever made, NO MATTER how terrible, shameful, stressful, or painful, you've paid your dues to be successful in the face of adversity, when either people, places, or things tried to steer you away from the King or Queen that you have always been by God's standards!

1 Peter (1:7) says, "These have come so that the proven genuineness of your faith of greater worth than gold, which perishes even though refined by fire-it may result in praise, glory and honor when Jesus is revealed." The context of this scripture is that God allows trials, so we can discover our weaknesses and his strengths as well as the infinite power of his grace and mercy!

"To fight and conquer in all of your battles is not supreme excellence; supreme excellence consists of breaking the enemies' resistance without fighting."

-Sun Tzu

Our self-worth determines our net worth of euthanistic pricelessness! Not to be represented by Amerikkka's statistics such as prison sentences, the NUMBER of words that are used to criticize us minorities, the NUMBER of negative thoughts we have had condemning ourselves, the NUMBER of partners we have hurt or have hurt us, money, cars, jewelry, places, breathes we have taken or heartbeats... These COST's are MORE THAN NUMBERS, and we are more than THE COST of our failures! WE ARE THE BLACK PRIVILEGED OF THE MOST HIGH! Finally, I was blessed with the sumptuous opportunity to engage in an intellectual conversation with my mother over the phone just about a year prior to writing this book. Considering my positive accomplishments and higher education, by happenstance, she mentioned aloud, "I got my son back!" I was so thrown aback by this statement that I found it sort of enchanting... I was stuck in my cognitive response, and in the affirmative. I asked my mother to repeat what she said, and to my heart, the euphoric enclosure of her words repeated, "I finally have my son back after almost 30 years!"

It is said that God did not make tear ducts for nothing. So... I utilized them in entirety out of pure joy, and I cried! And with every additional accomplishment, still I get emotional. My change, effort and caring has been a main ingredient to problem solving that has built perseverance in who I set out to be naturally.

I have championed to revolutionize the way we transcend into Greatness from the ordinary. For example: Djoser (the right pronunciation for this name is, joe-sir), a third dynasty second King, inherited the throne as the son of Kha'sekhemwy and Queen Hapynyma'at, who ruled during an age where they witnessed advances in civilization on the Nile such as the construction of architectural monuments, agricultural developments, trades and the rise of communities. Djoser revolutionized the architectural structure of the pyramids; he used stone instead of bricks, and in his rule and reign for almost 2 decades, territories were consolidated and Nome's (a providence or administrative reign of ancient Egypt called "Sepat" in the Egyptian language) subdued.

I am Djoser! I am "Archimedes" (The wise one)! He may have been behind the construction of the first computer and was killed by Roman soldiers, because he would not stop working. I am the Angolians, Yorubes, Akan, and Ibos, also others who were present on slave trips to Amerikkka and experienced a common horror, unearthly moans, cries and piercing shrieks from the soul! We are the circle rituals of historical importance, with religious and cultural visions from Africans in the Congo to the nucleus of our hearts, minds and communities.

Who are you? Who am I? Remember this: "The impossibilities in our lives are breeding grounds for the possible!" So turn impossible into I AM POSSIBLE! Now that's how you become MORE THAN JUST A NUMBER!

Faith will counter the narrative you've been carrying your entire life! For faith is not a predication on your outcome; faith is the value of your outlook. In the Bible, Mark chapter 3, Jesus went into the synagogue, and there was a man with a shriveled hand. Now these people were looking for any reason to charge Jesus with some type of wrongdoing. Jesus being the all wise and community/village provider, protector, healer and counselor, arrived to heal the man. The Pharisees asked Jesus if it was lawful to heal the Sabbath. Now,

Jesus was no chump. His witty and logical response to them was, "If any of you has a sheep and it falls into a pit on the Sabbath, will you take hold of it and lift it out? How much more valuable is a person than a sheep?" He then went on to tell the man to stand up. Now...I assume that Jesus telling the man to stand was to have confidence and faith in the midst of those who looked down upon him, shunned him and mistreated him because of disfigurement and indifference with the shriveled hand.

Jesus asked him to stretch out his hand. Now again...in the modern times, many brothers or sisters with this sort of defect would probably discreetly tuck their hand in their pocket or hide it in some way to evade imbecilic comments or thoughts from others. But when he stretched it out, he was completely healed. When Jesus left this place, an enormous crowd followed him, and he healed all who were ill. The sad part is that, because Jesus had done good, the Pharisees began to condemn him and plot to kill him.

The moral of the above story is that, whether you are a Christian, Muslim, Buddhist, Atheist, Black, Hispanic, Asian, white, rich, poor, prisoner, working citizen, etc., we all have shriveled up hands (flaws and defects) that cripple our self-worth and confidence, or even our decision making. This can be a physical, emotional, psychological, or spiritual trait. Therefore, contingent on your Higher Power, you will never overcome the shame of your flaws or defects if in fact tou don't stick your hand out so it can receive its necessary help. There's this saying that goes, "Go out on the limb. That's where the fruit is."

As in the illustration of Jesus, he doesn't want your good hand; he wants the bad one. Don't be ashamed of who you are, how you feel... The only way your Higher Power can do for you is if you believe that He can!

To hell with what anyone thinks of you or how they view you. REP YOUR SCARS! You don't need the applause of others; only the applause of the Higher Power!

People fear what they don't understand and hate what they can't conquer!

"To all those who are forgotten or think they are forgotten; it is in remembering who we are that we can become who we want to be!"

-Gloria Nouri

Let's begin to stop allowing circumstances to write our stories and create our realities! True repentance is deeply grounded in whom that was tested and survived. We benefit not if we continue to hold onto these seeds in our pockets along with that shriveled hand. What are we hiding from? from who? Go out on that limb and plant the seeds!

There is a glorious harvest and gifts of freedom awaiting our arrival, the fruit of who we really are that will counter all the reasons that we've ever doubted ourselves, our authentic worth in a legacy and historical lineage that wrote our stories for us. We just have to commemorate those facts and use the tools to build on it!

SEVEN LAWS OF LIFETIME GROWTH

1.) Always make your future better than your past.

2.) Always make your contribution bigger than your reward. 3.)

Always make your learning greater than your experience.

4.) Always make your performance greater than your applause.

5.) Always make your gratitude greater than your success.

6.) Always make your enjoyment greater than your effort.

7.) Always make your confidence greater than your comfort.

-Strategic Coach.com

I am finally proud to express that, the failures in my life freed me from my fear to change, to be different; to be me... A man of the most high!

Being forthright in my redemptive 180 turn around, with prayer and the prayers of my family and companion, I began to develop the strength in my body to explain these larger elements from this social, economic and racial human struggles that we have faced and still face today In this upcoming analogy, it places things in their right perspective pertaining to the Creator's wonderous design of the human body, which there are 200 types of tissues with 60 trillion cells that are aligned in perfect order. Muscle tissue contains hundreds to thousands of what is called Myofibrils and spender threads stacked length wise in muscle fiber, running the entire length of the fiber. There are actually bundles of tiny contractile protein filaments. The function of a Myofibrils illustrates the effects of various stresses, a kind of physical conflict, which these fibers must endure in order to develop property.

In going forward, skeletal muscle is made up of thousands of cylindrical muscle fibers bound together by connected tissue, through which blood vessels and nerves run through.

The number of fibers is probably fixed early in life, and each is designed for growth. Now... Myofibrils are set within a muscle for the purpose of strengthening the muscle as the person grows. With usage, these Myofibrils become stronger, but without exercise, they will atrophy. Follow me so far? The best part: when excess weight and pressure is put on a My fibril, it will expand, causing Edema or swelling. Nevertheless, although some portions will break down, there will be a rebuilding process where new strength is gained. Knowing just how much exertion to place on a muscle, results in the greatest degree of strengthening. So it is the stretching movement and exercise that creates muscle tension, placing pressure on the muscle system, which is imperative for healthy growth and development. And here's the anchor...without this physical struggle that we go through, muscles would atrophy and normal movement of the body would not be possible.

Therefore, in the same way that the larger struggles of life in any form becomes a positive means of growth and strengthening of our characters, without which we would continually weaken and atrophy in the face of life challenges!

Yes... I hear the cries rise up out of your souls, expressing "Enough is enough..." When will it stop? or when will it get better?

In the Bible, Paul, a servant of God, who is named Saul used to persecute Christians (kill, torture and oppress), however, he ended up totally changing his life in repentance and began to serve God with a pure heart. As well, in 2 Corinthians (12:7 9), he stated, "A thorn in the flesh was given to me, a messenger of Satan to buffet me-I pleaded with the lord 3 times that it might depart from me. And he said to me, 'My grace is sufficient for you, for my strength is made perfect in weakness'..."

In support of the above scripture, the thorn in the flesh portrays the fact that we all struggle with conditions in life that we may perceive as hardships, stresses and burdens. But what we must realize is that, in our weakest moments when all is dark, we must transcend what evil tends to destroy into championships out of hardships! Formulate strengths from stress, because pressure busts pipes and polishes stones into diamonds. Therefore, we have the upper privilege and freedom to choose our burdens!

Then and only then... we can break the oppression, depression and suppression from not only within ourselves, but in our men, women and children from this emotional, mental, physical, financial and institutional stigmatic snowball that continues to us minorities in our villages!

I plead and bleed my heart in between these paper's lines to whom has given up their hard-earned money to purchase this book, to look within themselves even if you have already done so pay it forward in action... stand in solidarity with me to spread the gift of positivity, effort, team work, care, concern, perseverance, problem solving, confidence, common sense, initiative and responsibility in reconstructing the fabrics of humanity! Never no shame! REP YA' SCARS! There is only one way from the bottom, and that is to the top as long as we are living and able. Understand that, nothing doesn't come to a sleeper but a dream, and if we don't take an active role and (or) change our lives, TIME will change it for us! Whether prison or free, do not allow Amerikkka and her cronies dictate THE COST of our worth!

Our feelings don't have intellect, we must bounce them off of the truth of this realistic and statistical mess that surrounds our community, our families, our strives and our peace.

Our ways of handling life's issues alone have to be readily eradicated as soon as possible! I mean, no Black or Hispanic man, woman or child, can for any considerable or reasonable period of time, wear one face to themselves and another to the multitude of others without finally getting bewildered as to which may be THE TRUTH!

Amerikkka... and even our own kind are blatantly telling us that She is always right; that its caste system was alleged to be our atrocious and harsh reality, and if we proceed to shut our eyes to itonly at our peril-if we do not rise up to this long-standing pernicious enemy (In-A-Me) and all His and Her dark powers... This enemy, my Kings and Queens...will come up from behind us one dark day and destroy us in total while we are facing the other day(s).

Our historic determinism that has been indigenously primitive in respect to authetistic and pure Black Privilege: THE COST OF OUR ROOTS IS BEYOND MORE THAN JUST A NUMBER!

WHO AM I??? (PART 1)

I AM A PRESTIGIOUS AFRO-AMERICAN KING, AND I REIGN SUPREME IN EVERY SETTING THAT I FIND MYSELF IN!

WHY??? BECAUSE THAT IS JUST WHO I AM...

I AM THAT MAN THAT MANY FEAR, BUT ALSO WANT TO BE.

I AM THE HERO AND THE VILLAIN, THE DREAM AND THE NIGHTMARE; THAT IS ME...

I HAVE WITHSTOOD THE BURDENS OF HARDTIMES AND CAME OUT ON TOP OF ALL ADVERSITIES,

AND I AM ONLY A FEW YEARS OLD, BECAUSE THE DAY THAT I FOUND MYSELF WAS ACTUALLY THE BIRTH OF ME...

I AM AN INTELLECTUAL WITH MUCH TO OFFER MY PEOPLE.

I WAS BROUGHT ABOUT BY THE CAUSE OF THE STRUGGLE, SO YOU CAN SAY THAT I AM THE SEQUEL...

MY PEN IS MY GUN, THE INK IS MY AMMUNITION, AND THE PAD IS MY TARGET.

I AM A POET, AN AUTHOR, MUSICIAN AND FREELANCE WRITER, AND I CAN APPEAL TO ANY MARKET...

CONFINEMENT HAS NOT HINDERED ME FROM ACHIEVING GREATNESS!

I'VE GAINED SO MUCH, A STRONG WILL, AN EDUCATION, AND MOST IMPORTANTLY, PATIENCE...

NOT ONCE DID I SIT AND THINK ABOUT ALL THE PRECIOUS TIME I HAD WASTED,

UNTIL I WAS IN THE COUNTY JAIL WITH A BOATLOAD OF TIME I WAS FACING...

I USED TO...LIVE BY THE GUN AND RESPECT THE JOUX.

I THOUGHT READING WAS FOR SUCKAS, SO I DIDN'T MESS WITH BOOKS...

BUT WHEN I FINALLY PICKED UP A BOOK, IT OPENED UP MY MIND!

I STARTED READING EVERYTHING, FROM SELF-HELP TO URBAN CRIME...

THAT'S WHEN IT DAWNED ON ME THAT AT ONE TIME I WAS BLIND.

I WAS PHYSICALLY AND FINANCIALLY INCLINED, BUT MENTALLY I WAS FAR BEHIND...

I THEN MADE A VOW TO MYSELF, TO NEVER AGAIN BE SUCH A CLOSE-MINDED FOOL!

I MADE THE DICTIONARY MY BEST FRIEND, STARTED STUDYING AND WENT BACK TO SCHOOL...

I AM A COUSIN, AN UNCLE, A SON, AND A BROTHER.

I AM A FRIEND TO A FEW AND A HOMIE TO OTHERS...

I AM ALL THAT I SAY I AM AND MORE!

I AM THAT AUTHENTIC MAN THAT EVERY WOMAN WANTS TO SHOW UP AT THEIR DOOR...

I AM THE EVER-PRESENT CONTROLLER OF MY EVERY SITUATION,

AND I AM GOING DOWN IN HISTORY AS ONE OF GOD'S GREATEST CREATIONS...

-K-BANG*

TABLE OF ICONS:

Common Sense: use God's judgment!

Confidence: I feel able to accomplish anything!

Effort: I'm willing to work hard, by any means!

Initiative: I'm positively engaging into action!

Caring: I have compassion for the village

Teamwork: I'm not only my brother's/sister's keeper! I am them!

Responsibility: I have to do what is right!

Motivation: I need to do it; get it done!

Perseverance: my finish is as strong as my start!

Problem Solving: All that I know into action! REP MY SCARS!

Acknowledgments

*Heavenly Father, thank you for giving me the strength to get through years of tribulations, no matter where I am today, you prepared a place for me with you to have the presence of your spirit today! Help me to help others, in the present as well as the future!

*DayQuan & Xy'Quan...my beloved sons; to truly understand something is to forgive it. Words cannot bestow the magnitude of everything you 2 endured through all of my faults and ignorance in this journey from my head to my heart. Being a shepherd didn't earn David much respect, but it prepared him to fight Goliath and eventually become Israel's greatest King! We may have been in an unbalanced circumstance, but God has prepared us for something unshakably great! Your Pop got y'all! Rashad, Rico & Rafiq...your unwavering faith will act as a rudder to keep you on course, so you'll reach your goals, plans and endeavors with a clear vision...

*Yazmin and Chriss McCallor, Ms. Cora and the rest of the Morris family: if God can take care of the means...the end will take care of itself! All my love, respect and prayers go out to y'all!

*Ivan Sr. & Renee, my brother in law and sister...thank you for your prayers and audacious fortitude! Our greatest freedom is the choice to choose our own freedom and destiny. You exemplify the meaning of MORE THAN JUST A NUMBER, not succumbing to the statistics.

*Rodney, Milton, Jordan and Mont...keep Dad's legacy and bloodline strong! Paula, Serita, Lonnie, Ciera...distance nor lack of communication will ever create a lack of love! I miss y'all! Mommom Benefield...thank you for your spiritual discipline as a child! That seed finally harvested my love! Aunt Shell...I miss and love you so much!

*My Aunt Deirdra...(lol!)...I'll say, my protector and angel who tried to keep her eyes on my wrongs to make them right. Thank You! Aunt Patti, my favorite and funny, loud life of the party aunt... Aunt

176

Cookie...pray with me; together we will fight against the restraints of the devil's noose... Aunt Jackie, Wanda and Wayne...God Bless Y'all...

*Uncle Kevin, my favorite uncle, who I envisioned being like, enjoyed being around when I was a kid; the thoroughest brother in the neighborhood, who I acquired my athletic and motorcycle interests from... Uncle June, I always admired your intellect and business idiocrasy...

*My cousins: Krissy, the only thing you have to offer another human being ever is your own state of being. You're more of a sister than a cousin. I love you cuzzo, and I'm proud of you! Shelly, progress is when your thoughts move in the same direction as your feet. I commend you on your walk of life. I love you cuzzo! Lana, life is what happens to you while you're busy making other plans. Thanks for your love and support when I needed your pure heart. You're an official rydah!!! Naman, stay focused and be who God created you to be! I feel your pain and understand you even if no one else does!!! D.J., Peace cuzzo! We hardly talk or see each other, but you remain in my prayers! Manny man, Tony, Nanny, Diamond, Trina, Tammy, Tiffany, kat, Vaginia, Poppy, Darlene and Val Seagar. My cuzzo Gerld. The Spencer, Baker and Miller family. The Huffington family. The Veney family. The Benefield family. The Love family. The Norman family...may we all continue to pray for reign, great health and prosperity...

*Kia and Gloria...the reward of patience is patience! I respect and praise you two. Thank you for my boys!!!

*My nieces and nephews...Jessica, Jarvis, Ivans Jr. and Ciara...I love y'all dearly...

*Maranetta...(lol!)...be who you are and say what you feel, because those who mind don't matter, and those who matter don't mind. God is God! Thank you for the shared space with you and allowing me to be God's Shepard with you!!!

*Wallace "Reality Childz" Battle...Some people aren't loyal to you; they're loyal to their need of you. Once their needs change, so does their loyalty! I can't explain the bond we have, brick and mortared through all of my tribulations in life. Thanks for your specific community of reliable others that you bring still after all these years- True Loyalty Is Love--Even when so many fake people turned their backs on me, you stood the test of time despite the fame you now have!

*K-Bang and Kaylee, my Pen In The Pen Family...when trust is present, when goals exist relatively vivid and endeavors are ultracritical, we rise from challenging situations--that's what successful people do--we get ahead of our past, copy all that is great, learn from it and realize the hardships only make us stronger and wiser! Thank you both for your endless efforts!

*HoviDough & K-Bang...in a few years we will be millionaires Bro!!! LOL!!! What they thought we would come to prison and just lay down in beds of mediocracy? I love y'all for you guy's intellectual and spiritual stabilities that enhanced my own! I'll meet y'all at the bank$$$

*Last but not least...I have to give R.I.P shout outs to Uncle Curtis, I miss you man! My Aunt Sheila, the world has missed your authenticity. I love you Auntie! My cuzzo Willy, I still can't fathom your passing!! I'll rep the bowling game for you! Uncle Buck! My boy Black Bobby...It's been 27 years since you've been gone. I never forgot as you see! Big Jack, Sheem, Steph, Slick, Mont-mont, Speedy, Sport, Naim and Ja'nae...

*Special R.I.P shout out to Christie N. Morris...tremendous woman of God, student, poet, author, singer, terrific mother and friend!!! Even though the sun has set, the stars still come my love!!! Thank you for your selfless authenticity that illuminated the gifts within me, which gave me a star role in God's elect. You always said, I can do it, and here is my first book. I love and miss you dearly!!!

*I also have to thank all of the supporters who purchased this novel! I hope you enjoyed the read. There are more books to come!

-D'Preme Norman

RECIDIVISM

RECIDIVISM IS JUST ANOTHER FORM OF GENOCIDE!

WE ROB AND KILL ONE ANOTHER, CONTRIBUTING TO THE SYSTEM'S MODERN DAY SLAVERY ENTERPRISE...

WE GO BEFORE THE JUDGE AND THEY BEGIN SPEAKING THIS FOREIGN LANGUAGE THAT WE CAN HARDLY IDENTIFY.

THIS IS WHY.... WE MUST MINIMIZE.... THIS SYSTEMICALLY CRAFTED GENOCIDE...

THIS IS "THE LAND OF THE FREE", WHERE YOU CAN BE ALL YOU CAN BE,

BUT THEY'LL FORCE SOME CUFFS ONTO YOUR WRISTS IF YOU SMOKE THE BUDS OFF THAT TREE...

WE ARE AT WAR WITH OURSELVES, AND I MEAN THAT FUGURATIVELY AS WELL AS LITERALLY.

WE CONSTANTLY BEAT OURSELVES DOWN, FAR BEYOND JUST MENTALLY AND PHYSICALLY...

IT'S EASY TO GET IN TROUBLE, BUT IT IS OH SO HARD TO GET OUT OF IT!

OUR BROTHERS SAY THAT THEY ARE REAL, BUT PROVE THROUGH THEIR ACTIONS THAT THEY ARE COUNTERFEIT...

IF AS A PEOPLE WE CAN'T UNITE, WE WILL NEVER WIN THIS FIGHT!

SO LOCK MINDS WITH YOUR FELLOW BROTHER, CAUSE THIS FIGHT IS FOR OUR LIFE...

AND WITHOUT EACH OTHER, WE'RE DESTINED TO FAIL. THIS TOPIC ISN'T A GAME.

YOU'LL BE CARRIED BY SIX OR THROWN IN A CELL; THEY'RE BOTH ONE IN THE SAME...

LOOK AT HOW THEY DIVIDE, THEN THEY CONQUER, PINNING US AGAINST EACH OTHER...

THE HOOD IS LIKE A BUNCH OF CRABS IN A BUCKET, EACH ONE PULLING DOWN THE OTHER...

WITH GUNS, DRUGS, WORDS AND ACTIONS, STOP FIGHTING WITH YOUR NEIGHBOR,

BECAUSE WE HAVE AN ABUNDANCE OF WORK TO DO, AND WE MUST ALL TAKE PART IN THE LABOR...

-K-BANG

D'PREME'S GLOSSARY:

adonize- to beautify or adorn oneself dissight- an eyesore; an unsightly or unpleasant object or prospect dolosity- deceit; hidden spite

ebullition- 1. a sudden, unrestrained expression of emotion 2. the state or appearance of boiling egregious- outstandingly bad, outrageous or shocking

enantiodromia- a process by which a strong force produces its opposite, and the interaction between the two exiguous- scanty, meager; insufficient facinorous- extremely wicked

fastuous- 1. proud, haughty, disdainful 2. pretentious, ostentatious, showy

flagitious- 1. deeply criminal; utterly wicked 2. infamous; scandalous; shamefully disgraceful hygeiolatry- an obsession with health or hygiene

hypothecation- a generic term for the use of property to secure a loan without transferring possession of the property; a pledge; a mortgage

inamorata (feminine) or inamorato (masculine)- a person who is loved; a lover indefesse- unwearied, untiring loogan- (US slang) a foolish or unsophisticated fellow

malversation- 1. corrupt behavior in a position of trust 2. corrupt administration, especially of public funds

matrilineal- a person or thing that was raised or established through a matriarchal lineage system paronomasia- a play on words; a pun patrilineal- a person or thing that was raised or established through a patriarchal lineage system prospicience- foresight; prevision solipsism- (philosophy) the theory that holds that self-existence is the only certainty, otherwise described as absolute egoism unasinous- being equal in stupidity undergrope- to delve into; to learn; to understand ultraneous- spontaneous; voluntary; of one's own accord

A PEN IN THE PEN PUBLISHING, LLC.

P.O. BOX 4092

LONG BRANCH, NJ 07740

WEBSITE: WWW.PENINTHEPEN.COM

FB: PEN IN THE PEN PUBLISHING / IG: PENINTHEPENPUBLISHING

ORDER FORM

NAME:_____ID#'S_____

INSTITUTION ADDRESS_____

CITY_____STATE_____ZIP_____

AVAILABLE TITLES: (ALL ARE $15.00)

THE COACH BY KBANG

SATANS PROPHET BY KBANG

21 SERVING 50 BY DAWAN INGRAM

SINCERE WORDS ARE NOT HARD TO FIND BY B. D. KELLAM

BREED OF UNCONTROLLABLE ELITE BY HAMZAH BROTHERS

BREED 2: THREAT OF THE SECRET 6 BY HAMZAH BROTHERS

YOUNG CANNON BY SADAAM HASAAN

SHIPPING CHARGES

FIRST BOOK $3.85

EACH ADDITIONAL BOOK $2.00

TOTAL $ _____

MAKE CHECK OR MONEY ORDERS PAYABLE TO:

A PEN IN THE PEN PUBLISHING, LLC.

ALSO AVAILABLE ON AMAZON, PAPERBACK, & eBook

ORDER FROM OUR WEBSITE: PENINTHEPEN.COM

FOR FASTER SHIPPING

A PEN IN THE PEN PUBLISHING, LLC.

P.O. BOX 4092

LONG BRANCH, NJ 07740

WEBSITE: WWW.PENINTHEPEN.COM

FB: PEN IN THE PEN PUBLISHING / IG: PENINTHEPENPUBLISHING

ORDER FORM

NAME:_____ID#'S_____

INSTITUTION ADDRESS_____

CITY_____STATE_____ZIP_____

AVAILABLE TITLES: (ALL ARE $15.00)

THE COACH BY KBANG

SATANS PROPHET BY KBANG

21 SERVING 50 BY DAWAN INGRAM

SINCERE WORDS ARE NOT HARD TO FIND BY B. D. KELLAM

BREED OF UNCONTROLLABLE ELITE BY HAMZAH BROTHERS

BREED 2: THREAT OF THE SECRET 6 BY HAMZAH BROTHERS

YOUNG CANNON BY SADAAM HASAAN

SHIPPING CHARGES

FIRST BOOK $3.85

EACH ADDITIONAL BOOK $2.00

TOTAL $ _____

MAKE CHECK OR MONEY ORDERS PAYABLE TO:
A PEN IN THE PEN PUBLISHING, LLC.
ALSO AVAILABLE ON AMAZON, PAPERBACK, & eBook
ORDER FROM OUR WEBSITE: PENINTHEPEN.COM
FOR FASTER SHIPPING

Made in the USA
Middletown, DE
23 November 2020

24972390R00109